Niger

Niger

BY ANN HEINRICHS

Enchantment of the World
Second Series

Children's Press®

A Division of Grolier Publishing

NEW YORK   LONDON   HONG KONG   SYDNEY
DANBURY, CONNECTICUT

Frontispiece: Young Wodaabe women watching male dancers

Consultant: Adeline Masquelier, Ph.D., Associate Professor, Department of Anthropology, Tulane University

Please note: All statistics are as up-to-date as possible at the time of publication.

Visit Children's Press on the Internet: http://publishing.grolier.com

Book Production by Herman Adler Design

Library of Congress Cataloging-in-Publication Data

Heinrichs, Ann
    Niger / by Ann Heinrichs.
      p. cm. — (Enchantment of the world. Second series)
    Includes bibliographical references and index.
    Summary: Describes the geography, plants and animals, history, economy, language, religions, culture, and people of Niger.
    ISBN 0-516-21633-3
    1. Niger—Juvenile literature. [1. Niger.] I. Title. II. Series.
DT547.22 H45 2001
966.26—dc21   00-021243

Acknowledgments

I am grateful to Irma Turtle of Turtle Tours for her sensitive guidance through Niger; to Joel Mayer and his Kakaki website readers for their insights and research assistance; and to the people of Niger for their warmth, hospitality, and goodwill.

Cover photo:
A village woman

Contents

Desert sand dunes

A Hausa woman

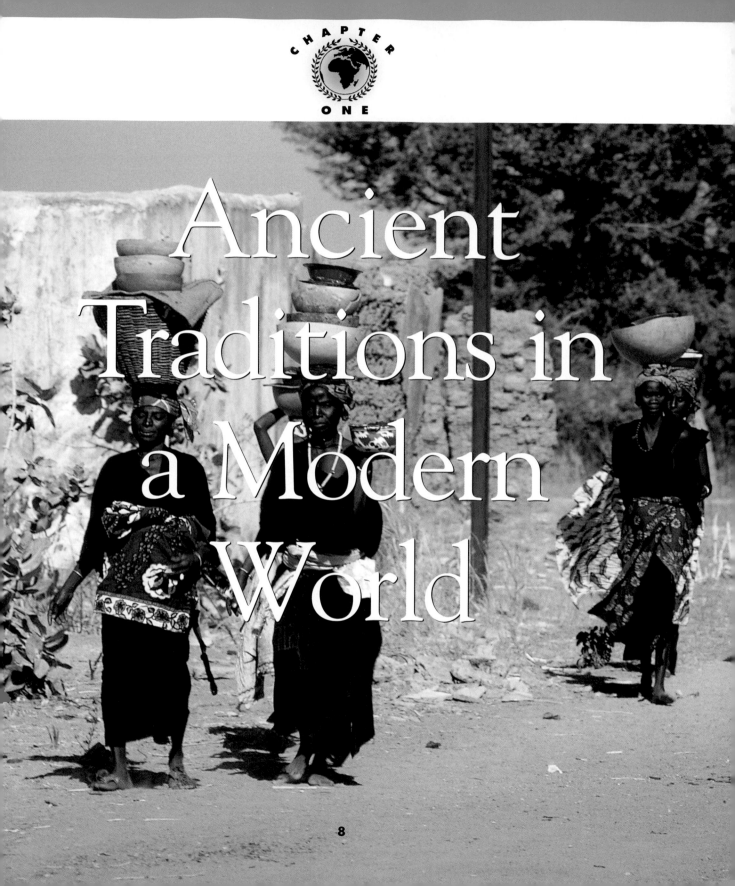

Ancient Traditions in a Modern World

F ATI FINGERS THE GOOD-LUCK AMULET IN HER POCKET AS she rides the school bus home. Her mother slipped the tiny packet into her pocket this morning as they kissed good-bye. "It will bring you luck on your exam," she whispered. Now Fati must wait most of the summer to see if she passed. If she did, she'll be able to enter secondary school in the fall. Meanwhile, she looks forward to a summer of reading and going to the swimming pool with her friends. But first, she's taking a little trip.

Fati and her family live in Niamey, the capital city of Niger in West Africa. They enjoy the conveniences of modern life—a life very different from the one Fati's parents left behind. Every summer, they send Fati to the country to spend a couple of weeks with relatives. While she loves to see her cousins, Fati does not believe she could live their way of life.

In the village, everyone gets up early in the morning for prayers. Then Fati helps her uncle's wives fix millet porridge for breakfast. After the meal, she helps pound millet for the noonday meal. She pours millet grains into a wooden mortar that's so tall it almost reaches her waist. Then she takes a heavy wooden club and pounds

Opposite: **Women on the way to market near Niamey**

Young girls pounding millet

Milking cows is one of many tasks that fill the day.

the millet to remove the husks from the kernels. Milking the cows and goats and preparing the meals keep them busy for the rest of the day.

Fati's great-grandfather founded the village, and all the children there are cousins of some kind. Because Fati's uncle is the oldest member of the extended family, he is the village chief. He portions out the farmland to each household and makes all marriage decisions. Fati's favorite cousin, who is also fourteen years old, is to marry very soon. Uncle believes it's high time Fati was married, too. When she says she wants to go to the university, Uncle just shakes his head.

After dinner, Fati takes a walk through the darkening woods. She loves the clean smell of the air, the cries of the birds overhead, and the sounds of little animals scurrying in the brush. She picks a bouquet of purple flowers and wonders how her school friends are spending the summer.

All of a sudden, a snake slithers by. Startled, Fati starts to shriek. Then she remembers what her grandmother says. The snake is the family's spirit protector—it will never harm a family member, and everyone should treat it with respect. But Fati is not so sure, and she breathes a sigh of relief when the snake disappears into the tall grass.

The distant cackle of a hyena sends shivers down Fati's spine. It reminds her that she had better get back to the village compound. Night is falling, and wild animals will soon be creeping about. Besides, the villagers say that witches roam around after dark looking for children to devour. Fati is not too sure of this, either. But just to be safe, she hurries toward the village's flickering fires.

A family in their modern home in the city of Zinder

Like Fati, the country of Niger exists in two worlds. One marches forward into modern society, while the other is grounded in age-old traditions.

Ancient religious beliefs are very much alive in Niger. They're animated with spirits who help, heal, or harm. At the same time, almost everyone follows the religion of Islam. Most men follow the Islamic practice of having several wives.

A Nigerien boy herding the family's goats

Others—especially college-educated men like Fati's father—prefer to have only one wife.

More than 80 percent of Nigeriens live in the rural countryside or on the desert fringes. Some live as nomads, herding their camels or cattle across the sparse grasslands. Most of the country is arid wasteland. The vast Sahara Desert covers the northern part of the country. City dwellers, like

Fati and her family, cluster in the south and the southwest, where the capital city is. Though some people enjoy a decent standard of living, Niger is one of the poorest countries on earth.

Niger has been overlooked by the Western world for most of its history. Just try asking anyone where Niger is. Most likely, they have never even heard of it. Nor would they know that Niger is one of the world's top suppliers of uranium.

Some of Africa's greatest empires reigned over the land that is Niger today. Their trade networks of camel caravans fanned out across the barren desert wastes—regions where Europeans could scarcely have survived. Long before the first colonists settled on American shores, West African empires had money, courts of law, complex music and literature, and fabulous mosques and universities.

Few people outside of Africa knew this was going on. Europeans first sailed to West Africa's coast in the 1400s, but it took them almost 400 years to penetrate as far inland as Niger. As European powers scrambled to carve up Africa for themselves, Niger became a colony of France.

Like most African nations, Niger has had a rough time emerging into the modern world. The country is home to more than half a dozen ethnic groups. They've learned to live together from centuries of contact through the caravan trade routes. Nevertheless, tribal rivalries and military takeovers have gotten in the way of peace and progress.

In spite of their differences, most Nigeriens believe in a democratic government that represents everyone's needs. That vision remains the hope for the nation's future.

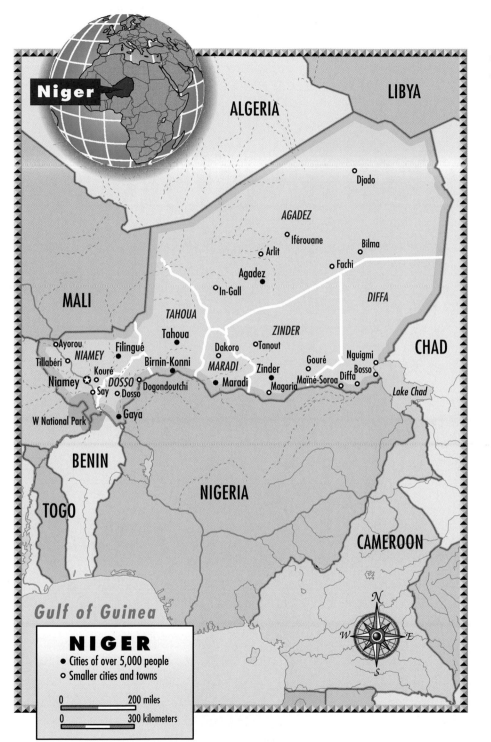

Niger

ALGERIA

LIBYA

Djado

AGADEZ

Iférouane

Bilma

Arlit

Fachi

Agadez

MALI

In-Gall

DIFFA

TAHOUA

Tahoua

Dakoro

ZINDER

Tanout

Ayorou

NIAMEY

Filingué

Birnin-Konni

MARADI

Zinder

Gouré

Nguigmi

CHAD

Tillabéri

Kouré

Maradi

Maïné-Soroa

Bosso

Niamey

DOSSO

Dogondoutchi

Magaria

Diffa

Say

Dosso

Lake Chad

W National Park

Gaya

BENIN

NIGERIA

TOGO

CAMEROON

Gulf of Guinea

N

W   E

S

NIGER

- Cities of over 5,000 people
- Smaller cities and towns

0   200 miles

0   300 kilometers

The Beauty
of the Land

ENDLESS STRETCHES OF SAND DUNES, BLACK VOLCANIC mountains, parched terrain with scattered tufts of grass, lush oasis villages with tall, graceful palms—all of these landscapes are part of Niger's natural beauty. Niger is a country in West Africa. It lies in the great, rounded "hump" of Africa that juts out into the Atlantic Ocean.

Niger's neighbors to the north, Algeria and Libya, both enjoy a long coastline along the Mediterranean Sea. Nigeria, along most of Niger's southern border, reaches south to the Gulf of Guinea, part of the Atlantic Ocean. Long, narrow Benin, another neighbor to the south, faces the Atlantic, too. But Niger is landlocked—completely surrounded by land. Chad (east of Niger), Mali, and Burkina Faso (to the west) are also inland countries.

Niger is the largest of all the West African countries. It's larger than the states of Texas and California together. And it's more than twice the size of France, its former colonial ruler. But in spite of its huge landmass, Niger is sparsely populated. That's because most of the country lies within the great Sahara Desert.

The Beauty of the Land **15**

A modern camel caravan crossing the Ténéré Desert

The Sahara

The Sahara is the largest desert in the world, covering more than 3.5 million square miles (more than 9 million sq km) of northern Africa. Its name comes from the Arabic *as-sahra*, meaning simply, "the Desert." In Niger, the Sahara covers all but the southern one-third of the country.

The most desolate reaches of Niger's Sahara are in the eastern half of the country. This region is called the Ténéré Desert. It stretches from the rocky plateau of Manguéni in the northeast to the Lake Chad basin in the far southeast.

Thousands of camel caravans once snaked their way across the burning sands of Niger. They carried salt and spices, green

West Africa

The nations of West Africa were once colonies of France. They were joined into a federation called French West Africa in 1895. Most of them became independent republics by 1960. West Africa today encompasses the following countries: Benin, Burkina Faso, Gambia, Ghana, Guinea, Guinea-Bissau, Ivory Coast, Liberia, Mali, Mauritania, Niger, Senegal, Sierra Leone, and Togo. The offshore islands of Cape Verde—once Portuguese colonies—are often considered part of West Africa, too.

tea from China, and dates from Arabia, as well as grain, copper, and gold. Niger's caravans still ply their trade today, though on a much smaller scale.

Parts of the Sahara are like a vast, empty sea of sand stretching to the horizon. In some places, chains of towering sand dunes cover the landscape, rippling and shifting in the hot winds. These areas are called *ergs*. The Great Bilma Erg of Niger's Ténéré Desert stretches eastward all the way into Chad.

These hauntingly beautiful sandscapes make up only part of the Sahara, though. Only about 15 percent of the Sahara is sandy. Other areas—called *regs*—are broad plains covered with gravel and stones. There are also rock-covered plateaus (*hamadas*) and high, rocky mountain ranges.

Lush oases flourish in the desert where underground water breaks to the surface in springs and wells. The oasis town of Bilma is Niger's easternmost town of any size. Salt caravans still travel there, as they have for centuries, citrus trees flourish, and palm trees wave over tropical flowers and shrubs.

High Places

In the center of Niger's Sahara region, the Aïr Mountains rise sharply above the desert floor. (*Aïr* is pronounced in two

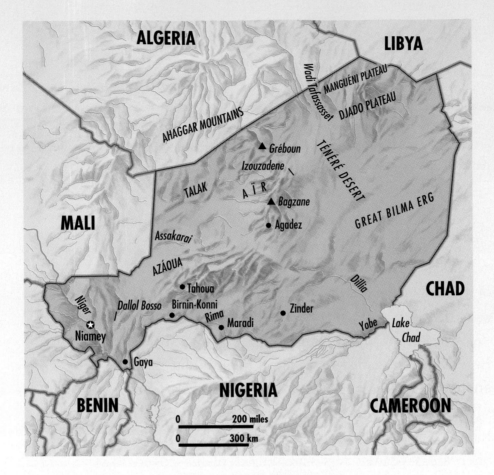

Geographical Features

Highest Elevation: Mount Gréboun, 6,378 feet (1,944 meters) above sea level

Lowest Elevation: Along the Niger River, 656 feet (200 m) above sea level

Longest River: The Niger River, Africa's third-longest river, flows for about 350 miles (563 km) through Niger.

Only Lake: Lake Chad, Africa's fourth-largest lake, covers Niger's southeastern corner.

Largest Desert: The Sahara covers two-thirds of Niger; the world's largest desert, it covers 3,500,000 square miles (9,065,000 sq km) of northern Africa.

Highest Annual Precipitation: 22 inches (56 centimeters) in the southern savanna

Lowest Annual Precipitation: Less than 7 inches (18 cm) in the desert near the Aïr Mountains

Highest Average Temperature: 122°F (50°C) in the daytime in the desert

Lowest Average Temperature: 32°F (0°C) or lower at night in the desert

Longest Shared Border: With Nigeria, 930 miles (1,497 km)

Greatest Distance North to South: 825 miles (1,328 km)

Greatest Distance East to West: 1,100 miles (1,770 km)

syllables: *ah-EAR*.) The Aïr Mountains are a treacherous jumble of rocky outcroppings, craggy peaks, high plateaus, and barren, rock-covered hills. Dramatic escarpments—long, steep cliffs—loom high above the sandy beds of ancient seas. Some sheer rock faces bear ancient engravings by prehistoric people.

Nestled in the valleys are lively oasis towns. In these lush, green villages, camels have plenty of water to drink between their desert treks. Outside of the oases, there are no permanent water flows—only streams that fill during the rainy season, and an occasional pool among the rocks. In the far north of the Aïr is Mount Gréboun, Niger's highest point.

For hundreds of years, the Aïr region has been the domain of the Tuareg people. Long known as fierce warriors and powerful merchants, the Tuareg still dominate the region. Agadez,

A Tuareg settlement in the Aïr Mountains

the Tuareg capital in the Aïr, was once a great crossroads for trade in the Sahara. Today, Agadez is one of Niger's largest cities.

Beyond Agadez, Tuareg nomads make camp and herd their camels, and scattered Tuareg villages dot the valleys and plains. Rich uranium deposits are found on the western edge of the Aïr Mountains. Mining operations in the region center around the city of Arlit (*ar-LEET*).

In Niger's far northeast is the Djado Plateau. Hidden among its exotic rock formations are mysterious rock engravings. Long-dead civilizations carved these animal pictures in a time when the desert was teeming with life. Here, too, lie the ruins of ancient villages.

Seasonal rains have brought life to this valley near Tahoua in the Sahel.

The Sahel

Southern Niger is in the heart of Africa's Sahel region. *Sahel* means "shore" in Arabic. If the Sahara is a vast sea of sand, the Sahel is the seashore. It's a transition zone between the Sahara to the north and tropical West Africa to the south.

Much of the Sahel is a great savanna, or grassland, with tall, leafy shrubs and sparsely scattered trees. Most of Niger's population lives in

The Aïr and Ténéré Natural Reserves

The Aïr and Ténéré Natural Reserves cover much of the Aïr Mountain region and the western part of the Ténéré Desert. The dramatic landforms of the Aïr range from rocky mountain masses and volcanic formations to the marble Blue Mountains at Izouzadene and the white marble hills at Kogo.

The adjoining portion of the Ténéré is one of the largest "sand seas" in the Sahara, with some of its highest sand dunes. Interspersed among dune fields are flat plains of gravel and stones.

A portion of the Aïr is a sanctuary for the addax, a rare type of antelope. Other large animals include gazelles, Barbary sheep, and wild sheep called aoudads. Jackals and foxes are common in the mountains, and baboons and monkeys survive in isolated spots.

The Aïr holds many relics of early human civilizations. Rock engravings from thousands of years ago depict long-vanished elephants and giraffes (photo). There are ancient tombs dating from a time before Islam arrived, as well as ruined villages with houses dating from the eleventh century.

The United Nations lists this entire reserve as a World Heritage Site—a place worthy of protection for all humanity. It's the largest natural reserve in all of Africa.

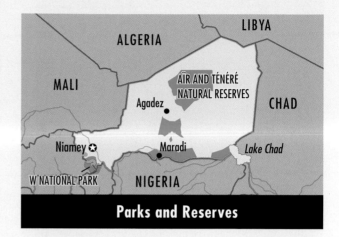

Parks and Reserves

Looking at Nigerien Cities

Zinder (above), located in the middle of southern Niger, is the country's second-largest city. It was founded during the 1400s as a stop on the trans-Saharan caravan route. In the 1700s, Zinder became the capital of a Muslim dynasty. French troops occupied the city in 1899, and from 1922 to 1926, it served as the capital of the French colony of Niger. Today, the historic Birnin Quartier has narrow streets, examples of Hausa architecture, the Grand Mosque, and the Sultan's Palace. The main population of Zinder belongs to the Hausa ethnic group. Many of them are skilled leatherworkers and dyers who produce traditional handicrafts. On land around Zinder, Hausa farmers grow much of Niger's groundnut (peanut) crop. Factories in the city process groundnuts and millet.

Maradi, located southwest of Zinder, is another Hausa town. It is Niger's third-largest city and lies just 31 miles (50 km) from the border with Nigeria. Maradi is also a major point on the highway across southern Niger. In 1945, flooding from a usually dry riverbed destroyed the town, and it was rebuilt at a higher elevation. Today, Maradi serves as a major market for Niger's farm goods. The Maradi Training Center helps farmers by supplying seeds and fertilizers and by providing information about farming methods. Peanut and cotton processing and leather tanning are Maradi's main industries.

Tahoua, Niger's fourth-largest city, is northwest of Maradi. It is a major stopping point on the road between Niamey and Agadez. Tahoua lies on the border between Niger's cultivated farmland and its pastureland where livestock graze. Farmers and herders come together at Tahoua's Sunday markets.

Agadez (below), Niger's fifth-largest city, is a Sahara oasis northeast of Tahoua. Tuareg people founded the city in the 1400s. It remains a center for Tuareg herders and is the home of their sultan. Visitors enjoy the town's camel races and the architecture of the Grand Mosque and the Sultan's Palace. In the *Vieux Quartier* (Old Section), leatherworkers and jewelers craft objects for sale. Today, Agadez also serves as the gateway city to the Aïr Mountains and the Ténéré Desert and as a supply stop for trucks going to and coming from the uranium, tin, and coal mines.

the Sahel. Most of the country's farming takes place there, too—especially in the far south, along the border with Nigeria.

Sahelian cities have long been crossroads for trade with Nigeria. The major towns along this southern strip are Dogondoutchi, Birnin-Konni, Maradi, and Zinder. Tahoua, north of Birnin-Konni, is the main city on the road to Agadez. Nguigmi, on the banks of Lake Chad, is the easternmost Sahelian town.

Sahelian farmers grow millet (a grain similar to wheat), groundnuts (peanuts), cowpeas (black-eyed peas), cassava, cotton, sorghum, and rice. Cattle, camels, oxen, sheep, and goats graze on the Sahel's natural pastureland. Industries in the Sahel include mills for processing grain, cotton, and other crops. Some mining, cement making, and other industrial activities take place there, too.

Lake Chad, in the far southeast corner, is Niger's only lake. Thousands of years ago, it was a vast, inland sea. As the climate changed and the desert advanced, it shrank to its present size. Because of the heat and lack of rain, Lake Chad is shallow, with scattered patches of dry sand. The borders of Niger, Nigeria, Cameroon, and Chad come together in Lake Chad. Thus, the lake has long been an area of international border disputes.

Being on the fringes of the Sahara, the northern Sahel is in constant danger of becoming desert itself. The vegetation does not anchor the sandy soil well when there are high winds and occasional heavy rains. Overgrazing and overfarming also make it easier for the desert to advance.

The Niger River near Niamey

The Niger River is the third-longest river in Africa. Only the Nile and Congo rivers run a longer course. The Niger is also the twelfth-longest river in the world. The first Europeans to pass through present-day Niger were exploring the Niger River. It was quite a challenge at the time to find and travel its full course.

The two legs of the Niger River form almost a right angle. That could be why, for centuries, the river was mysterious and confusing to Europeans. Its unusual course has a simple explanation, though. In ancient times, the two legs were really two separate rivers.

Another river, the Yobe, forms a part of the Niger–Nigeria border in the southeast. Other small streams and rivulets meander through southern Niger. Many of them are *wadis*, or seasonal water courses. They may swell to flood level in the rainy season, leaving only a ditch behind when it's dry.

Along the Niger River

The Niger River cuts right through southwestern Niger. Almost half the population lives in this small section of the country. The main river towns are Ayorou, Tillabéri, and Niamey (*nee-ah-MAY*), the capital and largest city.

Fishing is common along the Niger River, for both home and commercial use. Around Tillabéri, the Niger's waters irrigate fields of rice. Farmers raise groundnuts (peanuts) along the river, too. The town of Dosso has a plant for processing groundnut oil.

Ayorou is known throughout the region as a market town. Every Sunday, people of dozens of ethnic groups converge there to buy and sell donkeys, spices, food, pots and pans, and colorful fabrics. Many arrive by boat on the river, while others come on donkeys or camels.

Many people travel to the Sunday market in Ayorou by boat.

A Land of Extremes

The Sahara is one of the hottest, driest places on Earth, and much of Niger shares this climate. Daytime temperatures in the desert can reach more than 120° Fahrenheit (49° Celsius). Temperatures are much "cooler" in the south. Niamey's average temperature is only 84°F (29°C).

People and livestock die during severe droughts in Niger.

It almost never rains in the desert. But grasses and crops can grow in the southern Sahel region, because that's where most of the rain falls. The city of Zinder enjoys about 22 inches (56 cm) of rainfall every year.

Droughts are Niger's worst natural disasters. Crops shrivel, cattle die, and thousands of people starve to death. Herders on the fringe of the desert move south during a drought. This puts an even bigger strain on the meager food and water supplies.

On the other extreme are the floods. During the rainy season, downpours can be so heavy that ponds and dry riverbeds overflow. Fields, roads, and even entire towns may be completely flooded. Every year, the rains leave thousands homeless.

The Yearly Cycle

Monsoon season—the rainy season—lasts from June through September. The parched earth soaks up the water, and dry riverbeds fill up and overflow. Farmers welcome the rain, for that's the time to sow their millet and sorghum. But monsoon season can be a bad time for travel because the dirt roads are often washed out. Once the rains are over, nomadic herders come together to celebrate the passing of another year, renew old friendships, and make marriage matches.

The weather stays hot and humid through November. For many Nigeriens, this is the most uncomfortable time of year. Accustomed to dry heat, they would rather deal with scorching desert air than the heavy humidity.

December, January, and February are cool and dry. January is the coolest month. In the south, daytime temperatures drop to the low nineties Fahrenheit (low thirties Celsius). In the desert, nights may even reach the freezing point.

Temperatures start to climb again in March, and the air gradually grows hotter and drier. March through May is the season for the *harmattan*. This is a hot, dry wind that blows down from the Sahara. The skies grow hazy and overcast as fine-grained sand and dust fill the air. Sometimes the dust blows lower, creating dust storms or a kind of fog, so that travelers can hardly see where they're going. May is Niger's hottest month. Then dark clouds begin to roll across the skies—a sign that the rains are coming again.

Creatures Great and Small

THOUSANDS OF YEARS AGO, NIGER'S DESERT FLOURISHED. Water coursed through rivers and gathered into lakes and pools. Many kinds of animals gathered around the streams and water-holes of northern Niger. Antelopes, oxen, graceful giraffes, and clumsy hippos came to drink in the shade of tropical trees.

Rocky plateaus and barren sands now cover the landscape where waters once flowed. But petroglyphs—ancient rock carvings—show us what life was like then. In the Aïr Mountains and the far-northeastern Djado Plateau, there are carved-rock pictures of giraffes, elephants, hippos, and many other animals that can only thrive near water supplies.

As the climate changed and the desert advanced, large animals gradually moved farther south. Wild mammals such as elephants, hippopotamuses, and lions used to be more wide-spread in southern Niger. But they have almost disappeared because of poaching (illegal hunting) and deforestation. As people clear trees for firewood and living space, animals lose the protective cover where they can make safe homes.

Today, no animals live in Niger's harshest desert regions. But where enough rain falls, there are foxes, jackals, hyenas, baboons, and snakes. Gazelles, antelopes, and Barbary sheep roam in the northern mountain region. Lions and elephants are an occasionally rare sight in the dense southern forests. Hippopotamuses, crocodiles, and manatees—aquatic relatives of the elephant—can be seen in the Niger River.

Opposite: **Barbary sheep live in Niger's northern mountains.**

W National Park

Parc National du W (W National Park) is the largest wildlife park in all of Africa. Located along the Niger River in the far southwest, the park spreads across the borders of three countries: Niger, Burkina Faso, and Benin. It gets its name—W (pronounced DOO-bluh-vay in French)—from the wavy double bend in the Niger River along the edge of the park.

Lions, leopards, and cheetahs roam the park's wooded savannas. Though they stay out of sight much of the time, they're most likely to show up around the waterholes in the early morning and late afternoon. Elephants, hippopotamuses, rhinoceroses, buffaloes, and crocodiles gather at the waterholes, too.

Herds of antelopes graze across the grassy plains, while baboons, warthogs, hyenas, and jackals lurk in the cover of the trees. Great flocks of exotic native and migratory birds find refuge in the park, and more than 350 species have been spotted there. Visitors must drive—not walk—through the park because of the free-roaming lions and other flesh eaters.

The Big Giraffes

In 1997, archaeologists in the deserts of Niger came upon the largest, most stunning rock-art giraffes ever discovered. Tuareg guides who led the scientists to the site called them simply "the big giraffes."

The giraffes were engraved in the Neolithic era—between 6,000 and 9,000 years ago—on the broad surface of a rocky plateau. The biggest giraffe measures almost 20 feet (6 m), with a smaller giraffe nearby. To protect the site, scientists did not reveal its exact location.

"We've been all over Africa, and the giraffe appears to dominate the art in most areas of the continent," says David Coulson, one of the archaeologists. "Whatever it was, the giraffe was thought to be possessed of special powers."

Only a century ago, giraffes lived throughout West Africa. But the last wild giraffes left in West Africa now live south of Niamey. This herd of about sixty giraffes survives in a dense thicket, living on grasses and acacia leaves.

Birds

Many bird species from Europe and Asia spend their winters in Niger's wooded and grassy savannas. Some birds even migrate within the savanna, moving between the northern and southern reaches of the grasslands as the rainy and dry seasons come and go. Around April and May, before the monsoons begin, they fly north, where they'll be safe from torrential downpours. Once the rains are over in September, they fly back to their freshly watered southern homes.

Some of Niger's predator birds take good advantage of the migrants. Warblers, called whitethroats, eat plenty of sugar-rich berries before they leave Niger. As the fattened and juicy birds take to the air for home, they fall prey to predators that are eager to feed their nestlings.

In spite of the heat and lack of water, some bird species thrive in Niger's desert. Desert larks live on spiders, insects, and small seeds. One lark species uses its long bill to probe into the sand for grubs and ant lions. Sandgrouse and wheatears are some other desert species.

West Africa's few remaining wild giraffes live in Niger.

Above left: **A weaverbird perched above its nest**

Above right: **A marabou stork**

Swallow-tailed kites are sociable birds of the Sahel. Several families may nest in the same thorny acacia tree. Flocks of fifty or more kites careen through the air, catching insects on the wing. Making quick swoops to the ground, they also snatch up lizards.

Weaverbirds use grass to weave nests that look like round or oval balls. On the side they weave a little tube for going in and out. One tree on the savanna may harbor dozens of weaverbird nests.

Vultures and marabou storks soar over the savannas and desert fringes on the lookout for carrion, or dead animals. The two species sometimes compete for food and will fight over a carcass. Both birds also eat small live animals and village garbage.

Ostriches Stay Cool

The ostriches of Niger's arid regions have a remarkable ability to survive in hot weather. They get rid of extra heat by panting, which uses their body's system of air sacs. This keeps their lungs from losing moisture in the hot, dry environment.

Ostriches' system of blood circulation protects them, too. While their bodies may become very hot, their heads remain cool. Other warm-blooded animals begin to suffer brain damage at dangerously high body temperatures.

Ostriches are the largest birds in the world, weighing more than 300 pounds (136 kilograms). They feed on berries, seeds, succulent plants, and small animals.

Rollin', Rollin', Rollin'. . .

Dung beetles are often seen skittering with their giant cargo across the arid savannas of the Sahel. These remarkable insects live on the food material they find in dung, or animal excrement. Around 7,000 species of dung beetle are found worldwide, and Africa has more of them than any other continent.

There are three types of dung beetle: dwellers, tunnelers, and rollers. Dwellers live inside dung heaps and make their nests there. Tunnelers dig burrows through the dung and make their nests in the ground beneath it.

West Africa's rollers fashion a chunk of dung into a ball. It can weigh up to fifty times as much as the beetle. They move the ball to their nest by running backward with their front legs on the ground and their back legs up high, rolling the ball.

This hardy shrub is typical of the tough, sparse vegetation in the Sahel.

Clumps of hardy grasses cover the broad savannas of southern Niger's Sahel region. Thorny bushes, succulent shrubs, and deep-rooted trees survive there, too. In the far south, where rains are the heaviest, there are even patches of dense woods. But forests cover only about 2 percent of Niger's land.

Farther north, nearer to the desert, the wooded areas give way to wide-open spaces. Here the tufts of grass become farther apart. Thorny acacia trees and thick-trunked baobabs are scattered across this semi-arid landscape.

Palm trees, ficus trees, and flowering tropical plants grow in Niger's moist southern regions. In the most densely wooded areas grow many beautiful trees, such as gao, tamarind, baobab, and mahogany.

Goats nibbling on the leaves of thorny acacia trees

In oasis towns such as Fachi and Bilma, there are date palms, eucalyptus trees, and fruit trees. People there can grow vegetables, maize (corn), and other grains.

Many kinds of acacia trees thrive in the dry savanna. Their thorns store water, and their crowns spread wide to capture the morning dew. Giraffes and camels nibble their leaves and birds nest in their branches.

The Monkey Bread Tree

Baobabs are among the largest trees in the world. They grow enormously thick trunks measuring as much as 30 feet (9 m) around. Baobabs live long lives, too. Some are believed to be more than 1,000 years old.

The baobab's nickname is the monkey bread tree. That's because baboons like to eat its pulpy fruit. In the age-old religion of Niger's rural countryside, a great old baobab is believed to be the home of powerful tree spirits.

Baobab trees have enormous trunks and may live to be very old.

In one southern village, an old man sits all day beside an ancient baobab. His role is guardian of the tree, and he has sat there for twenty years. His father, grandfather, and great-grandfather were guardians before him. Villagers bring gifts of food and perform ceremonies at the tree to appeal to the spirits for favors such as rainfall.

The Tree of the Ténéré

One acacia is the most famous single tree in all of Niger. Called the *Arbre du Ténéré* (Tree of the Ténéré), it was the last tree that remained of the great forests that once dotted the Sahara.

There it stood, in the bleak and desolate wasteland, about 250 miles (400 km) from the nearest tree. The Tree of the Ténéré was such a remarkable site that it was even shown on maps of Niger.

Standing about halfway between Agadez and Bilma, the tree was a landmark on the caravan route between the two cities—until 1973, that is. With thousands of square miles of desert before him, a truck driver accidentally ran into the tree and knocked it down. Today, a metal tree stands in its place, and maps still show its location. What remains of the legendary Arbre du Ténéré is now enshrined in Niamey's national museum.

Empires, Regimes, and Democracy

I F YOU LOOK AT THE BOUNDARIES OF NIGER TODAY, THEY tell you nothing about its centuries of history. These borders enclose no ancient kingdom and no single ethnic group. Instead, some of Africa's greatest empires spilled over into the territory that became Niger. Refugees from defeated kingdoms found a safe haven there, too.

Opposite: **Horsemen in an independence day celebration**

Prehistoric people may have lived in Niger tens of thousands of years ago. Ancient rock carvings in Algeria's Tassili N'Ajjer Plateau to the north depict farmers, herders, and hunters who lived in the region as early as 8,000 years ago. Their cattle resemble the long-horned Zebu that Niger's Fulani now herd. And some of the women's hairstyles even resemble those worn today.

Ancient rock carvings in Algeria's Tassili N'Ajjer Plateau

Masters of Saharan Trade

The Kanem and Bornu Kingdoms were among the earliest known governments in the area that is now Niger. They centered around Lake Chad, in the far southeast. These kingdoms were the domain of a powerful group of peoples in central Africa.

As early as the ninth century, the state of Kanem grew up on the northeast side of Lake Chad. Plagued by rivals, the

Kanem state collapsed in the fourteenth century. Its rulers simply moved to the west side of Lake Chad. By about 1600, this new empire—the Bornu kingdom—was one of the most powerful states in Africa.

Meanwhile, the Tuareg people came to dominate the central Sahara and the Ahaggar Mountains, in present-day Algeria. In the 1100s, they spread south into the Aïr Mountains of Niger. By the 1400s, the Tuareg were running trade caravans across that part of the Sahara. Salt from the oasis of Bilma was a major trade item, and Agadez became the Tuareg trading center and capital. The sultan of Agadez, who controlled the caravans, was the most powerful man in the entire region.

Pages of a ninth-century Koran from North Africa

Islamic Culture

By this time, the religion of Islam had spread from Arabia across northern Africa. Both the Kanem-Bornu kings and the Tuareg chiefs embraced the new religion by the eleventh century. Islam united its followers, called Muslims, in a common religious and cultural bond. Cities flourished with Islamic arts and architecture. Men and boys learned to read and write Arabic by studying the Koran, Islam's holy scriptures. Islamic principles inspired many facets of life, from business transactions to military conquests.

While the Tuaregs were settling into Agadez, other great empires held sway to the west of present-day Niger. Here in the Sahel region, on the southern fringe of the Sahara, were most of Africa's largest cities. They were crossroads for Saharan caravan routes as well as centers of Islamic learning.

Mali was the greatest empire in West Africa in the thirteenth and fourteenth centuries. Under Mansa Musa, who reigned from 1312 to 1332, the empire reached all the way into what is now southern Algeria and southern Niger's Hausaland. Mansa Musa brought Muslim scholars and artisans from Arabia to Mali. In the city of Timbuktu, he built the University of Sankore, which, together with the Sankore Mosque, became a great center of Islamic learning.

The Mosque of Sankore in Timbuktu, Mali

Ali the Great

Sonni Ali, also called Sonni Ali Ber, became king of the Songhai in 1464. He went on to build the powerful Songhai Empire and ruled it until his death in 1492. Sonni Ali's empire-building began when he conquered the great Mali city of Timbuktu in 1468. By taking the wealthy trading city of Jenné in 1473, he was able to control the region's trade.

Sonni Ali's kingdom became the most powerful empire in West Africa. He spent much of his reign fighting off attacks by neighboring tribes such as the Mossi, the Fulani, and the Tuareg. He adopted Islam, but he offended orthodox Muslims by combining Islam with practices of traditional Songhai religion. His name means Ali the Great.

The Songhai Empire

The Mali Empire began to decline after 1400, making way for Sonni Ali Ber. In 1464, this warrior-king came to the throne of Gao, a state with allegiance to Mali. (Today, Gao is a city on the Niger River just west of Niger's border with Mali.) In 1468, Sonni Ali mobilized his army and his fleet of warships on the Niger River. After conquering Timbuktu and other important Mali cities, he established the Songhai Empire.

Sonni Ali's successor, Askia Muhammad, expanded the empire even farther. Between 1493 and 1528, he conquered the rest of Mali, Hausaland, and many important oasis cities in the Sahara. Under Askia Muhammad, the empire had many levels of officials to run government business. Islamic law became the law

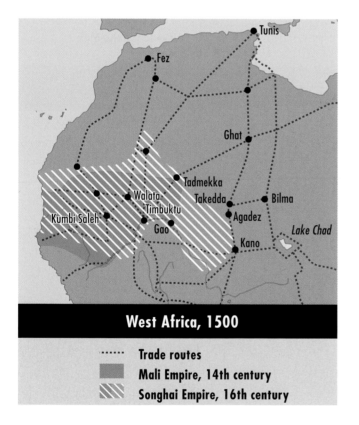

West Africa, 1500

..... **Trade routes**
▨ **Mali Empire, 14th century**
▨ **Songhai Empire, 16th century**

of the land, and Islamic culture permeated the cities. Successors continued with the expansion until the Songhai Empire became the largest kingdom in all of Africa.

But the Songhai were soon to meet a force they could not match   guns. Armed with muskets, an army from Morocco took the city of Gao in 1591. This put an end to the Songhai Empire, the last of the great empires of West Africa.

Some Songhai leaders escaped down the Niger River into today's Niger. There they found support and refuge among the Songhai and Djerma people.

Hausaland

Hausaland flourished in the area that is present-day Nigeria, spilling over into southern Niger. It stretched from the Niger River in the west to Lake Chad in the east.

At first, Hausaland was just a loose collection of farming villages and market towns. Hills throughout the region were holy sites, where priests performed religious rites for the surrounding communities. The priests were also guardians of sacred trees.

"He Will Not Be"

Askia Muhammad (died 1538) is sometimes called Muhammad Touré. He took over rule of the Songhai Empire in 1493 after defeating Sonni Ali Ber's son in battle. It is said that he gave himself the title *Askia* to make fun of Sonnis who said of him, "*a si tya*" ("he will not be"). In the 1500s, he brought the Songhai Empire to the height of its greatness. He championed "pure" Islam and made a pilgrimage to the holy city of Mecca in Arabia. Under Askia Muhammad, the Songhai Empire reached its greatest extent. His rule extended as far east as Agadez. But he was his best as an organizer and administrator. He standardized money, weights, and measures throughout the empire. Dozens of government departments oversaw finance, agriculture, forests and waters, justice, military training, and more. His tomb in Gao, Mali, is a holy shrine to this day.

**The city of Kano
in Hausaland**

According to Hausa tradition, seven great cities grew up in Hausaland. Unlike Songhai cities, which owed allegiance to Gao, the Hausa cities were independent city-states. We know the most about the city of Kano because of the *Kano Chronicle*, a written collection of legend, oral tradition, and historical events.

The Hausa cities grew into important centers for Saharan trade. Through traders, Islam began to reach into Hausaland in the 1300s. But traditional beliefs remained strong. While much of Hausaland accepted Islam, the people mixed in many of their traditional local beliefs.

Cattle herders, called the Fulani, began migrating into Hausaland in the 1450s. The Sahara kept advancing, and they were seeking good pastureland for their herds. Fervent Muslims, the Fulani set up Islamic schools in the Hausa cities. Gradually Islamic culture spread throughout Hausaland, just as it had in the Songhai Empire.

Over the next 300 years, the Fulani became ever more powerful in Hausaland. One after another, they transformed the Hausa kingdoms into Muslim states.

The Fulani and the Sokoto Caliphate

Hausaland met its downfall at last in 1804. The Fulani allied themselves with Usman dan Fodio, a powerful caliph, or Islamic governor, in northern Nigeria. Usman inspired the Fulani in a *jihad* (holy war) against the Hausa states. Hausaland fell, and its territory became part of Usman's Sokoto Caliphate.

Some of the Hausa kings escaped up to the northern fringes of Hausaland, in present-day Niger. They set up Hausa kingdoms in Maradi, Zinder, and other cities. There they carried on their traditional ways of ruling and their mixture of Islam and native religion. The royalty of Kano settled in Zinder, which became a major city along the Kano-to-Agadez trade route.

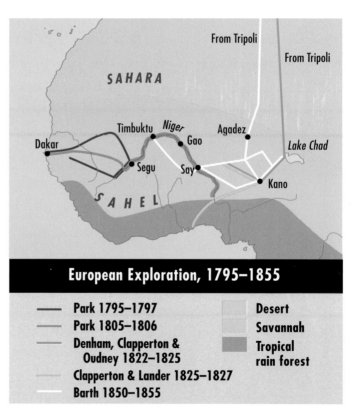

European Exploration, 1795–1855

—— Park 1795–1797	▢ Desert
—— Park 1805–1806	▢ Savannah
—— Denham, Clapperton & Oudney 1822–1825	▣ Tropical rain forest
—— Clapperton & Lander 1825–1827	
—— Barth 1850–1855	

European Explorers

Sailing ships from Portugal first reached West Africa's coast in the 1400s. But more than 300 years passed before Europeans penetrated as far inland as Niger.

Above left: **Mungo Park**

Above right: **Heinrich Barth**

A Scottish explorer named Mungo Park was the first European to pass through present-day Niger. He was one of dozens of explorers trying to trace the full course of the Niger River.

Park was the first to discover that the right-angled Niger was one river, not two, but he never lived to report the news. He never stopped along the river to ask local chiefs for permission to pass, and he never paid tributes or tolls. He just fired on anyone who looked threatening. In Niger, Park passed through Tuareg and Hausa territory. He finally met his end when he was attacked in Bussa, in present-day Nigeria.

Unlike many other Europeans, the German explorer Heinrich Barth genuinely liked and respected Africans. He traveled through Agadez in 1850 and the Lake Chad region in 1851, taking extensive notes on local cultures. He made a vocabulary list of Hausa words, calling it "the most beautiful, sonorous, rich and lively" of all the African languages.

By this time, Europeans had been taking advantage of Africa's human and material resources for many centuries. Portugal began buying slaves from West African slave traders in the 1400s. Africa's gold, spices, exotic wood, and slaves attracted many other European powers. Inevitably, they clashed in the struggle to claim chunks of Africa as colonies.

Europeans began buying captured Africans from slave traders in the fifteenth century.

French Colonial Rule

England, France, and five other European countries met in the Berlin Conference of 1884–1885. They agreed on how to divide Africa among themselves, and much of West Africa—including Niger—went to France.

The Berlin Conference of 1884–1885

French rulers and Africans in
French West Africa, 1910

In 1895, France united its West African colonies into a federation called French West Africa. It was ruled by a governor-general in Dakar, now the capital of Senegal. Niger became part of the federation in 1896. In 1898, an Anglo-French commission drew Niger's present-day boundaries.

France's greatest obstacles in Niger were the Tuareg. The Nigerien Sahara had practically belonged to them for 1,000 years. The Tuareg revolted against French colonial rule in 1906. For years, their frequent rebellions kept the French from turning Niger into a full-fledged colony.

Niger finally became an official colony of French West Africa in 1922. A Nigerien governor reported to the governor-general in Dakar, and local chiefs oversaw their territories within the colony. France did not invest much money or effort in developing Niger. No roads or railroads were built, and little was done to develop Niger's economy.

The Independent Republic

After World War II (1939–1945), France began the process of releasing its colonies. In 1946, the West African colonies became French territories and could send elected representatives to the French Parliament, or congress, in Paris.

Hamani Diori became Niger's first president when his political party won a majority in the 1958 elections. Diori set up a government and, with France's approval, the Republic of Niger declared independence on August 3, 1960.

Hamani Diori, Niger's first president

In 1971, with the aid of France, Diori began developing Niger's rich uranium deposits in the north. Modern mining operations built the city of Arlit into an important industrial center. But when drought and famine ravaged the Sahel region for five straight years (1968–1973), Diori could not cure Niger's problems. Even worse, Diori and his government ministers were found to be taking international food aid for their own profit. In 1974, Lieutenant Colonel Senyi Kountché led a military coup that toppled Diori's government.

Military Rule

Kountché set up a twelve-man military government. He banned political activities, suspended the constitution, and replaced the legislature with a national development council. As uranium brought more income into Niger, Kountché was able to spend more on social and economic programs and help the country recover from the drought. For a few years, the nation's economy flourished. But it took a nosedive in the 1980s when uranium prices dropped worldwide.

Kountché reduced the number of military officers in government positions and appointed a civilian prime minister. In 1987, just as a new constitution was about to go into effect, Kountché died. Colonel Ali Saïbou, the army chief of staff, succeeded him, and a new constitution was adopted in 1989.

The Tuareg Rebellion

Thousands of Tuareg herdsmen lost their animals in the drought of 1984–1985. Hoping for a better life, many moved north into Algeria and Libya. While they were away, they formed a Tuareg political party. They decided it was time to do something about decades of poor living conditions, loss of culture, and lack of political influence. Ali Saïbou invited the refugees back in the late 1980s, promising improvements in all these areas. Unfortunately, he was not able to deliver on his promises.

The Tuareg rebellion officially began in May 1990, when a group of Tuareg attacked a guardhouse at Tchin-Tabaraden, southwest of Agadez. Saïbou sent in soldiers, who massacred several dozen Tuaregs. The next few years were wracked by Tuareg attacks, counterattacks, and sporadic outbreaks of violence.

Meanwhile, other Nigeriens were clamoring for a democratic government. Security forces fired on university students who were demonstrating in February 1990. Saïbou won the presidential election of 1991, but he was the only candidate. That led to more violent demonstrations and another reorganization. A National Conference met in Niamey in July 1991. The conference took charge of

Mano Dayak

Mano Dayak (1949-1995) was an internationally known Tuareg leader. Born and raised in the Aïr region, he attended public school in Agadez and later studied at Indiana University and at the Sorbonne in Paris, France. He and his wife, Odile, set up a tourist business in Agadez in the 1970s. They took people through the Ténéré Desert and the Aïr Mountains, introducing them to Tuareg culture. A racing enthusiast, Dayak raced in several Paris–Dakar motor rallies.

Dayak had a charismatic personality and a strong vision for his people's future. He became a leader in the Tuaregs' fight against injustice and persecution, and led the *Front de Libération de Tamoust* (FLT) political party.

In 1993, after years of hostilities on both sides, Dayak negotiated a peace agreement between the Tuareg and the Niger government. He was on his way to Niamey for further peace talks in 1995 when his plane crashed near the Aïr Mountains.

the country, suspending the constitution, the legislature, and Saïbou's government.

Democratic Elections

Out of the conference came a new constitution and a plan for Niger's first democratic, multiparty elections. These 1993 elections were hotly contested. Candidates from twelve newly formed political parties ran for seats in the National Assembly. In the presidential race, it took two rounds of elections for Mahamane Ousmane to win by a very slim margin.

Ousmane did his best to put the country in order, but it was an uphill battle. Government spending was too high, and foreign aid had dwindled when the National Conference was in charge. Government employees went unpaid for months, and workers went on strike.

Under Ousmane, the government and the Tuareg rebels finally agreed to a cease-fire in 1994 and a peace accord in 1995. The last hold-out rebel group signed a peace agreement in 1997.

Ibrahim Baré Maïnassara

The Military Coup of 1996

Eventually, Ousmane and his prime minister became locked in such disagreement that the government could hardly function. In January 1996, Colonel Ibrahim Baré Maïnassara led a military coup that overthrew Ousmane's government. What happened next was nothing new for Niger. Maïnassara suspended the constitution, dissolved the National Assembly, and banned political parties.

Maïnassara promised to hold democratic elections and restore a civilian government. But he dissolved the independent commission that was to count votes in the July 1996 presidential election and put his four opponents under house arrest. Naturally, Maïnassara won the election. In protest, many Western countries withdrew their economic aid to Niger.

New Hope for Democracy

Maïnassara's term was wracked with political arrests, rebellions, deportations, unfair trials, and labor strikes. In April 1999, he was assassinated. A National Reconciliation Council took over, partly made up of those responsible for Maïnassara's death. At last, in October 1999, Niger held its first democratic elections since 1993. The victor was Tandja Mamadou.

Niger had enjoyed a taste of democracy, lost it for a few years, and won it back again. The country's political troubles will probably continue for many years to come. But one thing is certain—Nigeriens will never again be content without democracy.

Nigeriens voting in the 1999 presidential elections

How the People Rule

52

N IGER BECAME AN INDEPENDENT REPUBLIC IN 1960. Since then, the country has seen many leaders come and go. Almost every new government has changed Niger's constitution, its politics, and its balance of power.

There are two things Nigeriens have learned from all their political turmoil. First, they want to live in a democracy, where leaders are chosen by the people's vote. And second, they must have a true balance of power, so that no one person or group controls the government.

Nigeriens tend to identify more with their particular ethnic group than with their nation. They are more likely to say, "I am Hausa" or "I am Djerma," than they are to say, "I am Nigerien." Many younger people, however, are giving up their ethnic traditions in order to fit in with modern city life.

Opposite: **The sultan of Agadez riding past the city's mosque**

The National Flag

Three horizontal stripes run across Niger's national flag. From top to bottom, they are orange, white, and green. In the center of the white stripe is an orange circle. The orange stripe is a symbol for the Sahara. To Nigeriens, it is inviting all people to try to conquer its sandy expanse. White stands for the people's purity and innocence as they faithfully carry out their daily tasks. The orange circle represents their sacrifices for justice and human rights, and their determination to keep defending these rights. Green stands for the hope that rests in Niger's fertile land. If it is cultivated, Nigeriens will be stable and prosperous.

As in the United States and France, Niger has three branches of government—executive, legislative, and judicial. This is one way to have a balance of power, so that no one branch becomes too strong.

The Executive Branch

The president is Niger's head of state and chief executive officer. He is elected to a five-year term. After election, the president must choose the prime minister from the political

The Presidential Palace in Niamey

party with a majority of seats in the National Assembly. That party gives the president a list of acceptable candidates, and he chooses one from the list.

The 1999 constitution provides that the president and prime minister share the executive power. However, it has provisions for preventing a deadlock between the two. The president is the head of state, while the prime minister is the head of government.

To help him run the government, the president appoints a council of ministers. Each minister oversees one area of the country's operations. For example, Niger has ministers of agriculture and livestock, transport, defense, education, trade, and many more.

The Legislative Branch

An eighty-three-member National Assembly is the nation's legislature, or lawmaking body. Like the president, its members serve for five-year terms. Eight of the assemblymen are elected to represent various minority groups in Niger. The other seventy-five are elected from districts divided according to population. They run for office as members of a political party.

National Anthem

"La Nigérienne"
Words by Maurice Albert Thiriet
(Translated from the French)

By the waters of the mighty Niger,
Which adds to the beauty of nature,
Let us be proud and grateful
For our newly won liberty!
Let us avoid vain quarrels
To spare ourselves bloodshed,
And may the glorious voices
Of our race, free of domination,
Rise upward in one great surge
As high as the dazzling sky,
Where its eternal soul, watching over us,
Will make this nation greater still!

Chorus:
Arise! Niger! Arise! May our fruitful labors
Rejuvenate the heart of this ancient continent,
And may this song resound to the four corners
of the Earth
As the cry of a just and valiant people!
Arise! Niger! Arise! On land and on the waters,
To the rhythm of the swelling drum-beats' sound,
May we forever be united, and may each of us
answer the call
Of this noble future that tells us: Go forward!

We rediscover in our children
All the virtues of our ancestors.
These virtues are our inspiration
Through all our struggles.
We confront ferocious animals,
Most often scarcely armed,
Seeking only to live in dignity,
Not slaying with a lust to kill.
On the steppe where all feel thirst,
In the scorching Sahel,
Let us march tirelessly forward
As magnanimous and vigilant masters.

Chorus

The National Assembly building in Niamey

Rival parties compete fiercely to gain a majority of the seats in the legislature. Often, two or more parties merge to form a union, or coalition. That way, weaker parties can gain more power than they would ever have on their own.

An Uneasy Democracy

Mahamane Ousmane (left), Niger's first democratically elected president, took office in 1993. The Constitution at that time called for a "cohabitation" government, in which president and prime minister were equally powerful. But rivalry between Ousmane and Prime Minister Hama Amadou brought the government to a standstill. In 1996, Colonel Ibrahim Baré Maïnassara seized power in a military coup. Later that year, Ousmane lost the presidential race to Maïnassara in a fraudulent election. Ousmane continued to be intensely involved in Nigerien politics and was a candidate in the 1999 presidential election.

The Judicial Branch

Niger's system of laws is based on French civil law and on Nigerien custom. The Supreme Court is the nation's highest court and the head of the judicial branch of government. Another national court, the High Court of Justice, tries the president or any other high officials for crimes such as treason. It consists of seven permanent judges and three rotating judges. The 1999 constitution also established a Constitutional Court.

Niger's Court of Appeal hears cases appealed from lower Criminal and Assize Courts. Courts of First Instance, with many

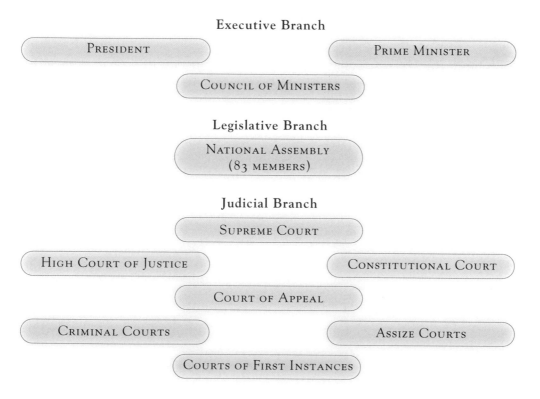

NATIONAL GOVERNMENT OF NIGER

Executive Branch

PRESIDENT

PRIME MINISTER

COUNCIL OF MINISTERS

Legislative Branch

NATIONAL ASSEMBLY
(83 MEMBERS)

Judicial Branch

SUPREME COURT

HIGH COURT OF JUSTICE

CONSTITUTIONAL COURT

COURT OF APPEAL

CRIMINAL COURTS

ASSIZE COURTS

COURTS OF FIRST INSTANCES

subdivisions for different types of crimes, try cases for the first time. One type of court within the first-instance courts are Labour Courts. There is a serious shortage of magistrates, or judges, to handle cases. Niger has one judge for every 40,000 people.

Political Parties

Political parties play an important role in Niger's process of government. It's often hard to keep track of them all. Special-interest parties form and re-form, ethnic groups form parties that often divide into several subgroups, and election time brings on last-minute coalition parties.

Enthusiastic supporters of a presidential candidate riding through the streets of Niamey

The parties are best known by their initials followed by a popular name that indicates their ideals. For example, Tandja Mamadou is the leader of the MNSD-Nassara party. MNSD stands for *Mouvement national pour une société de développement* (National Movement for a Society of Development), and Nassara is Hausa for "victory." Tandja Mamadou won the presidency in the 1999 elections.

Local Government

Niger is divided into seven departments and one capital district (Niamey, the capital). The departments are Agadez, Diffa, Dosso, Maradi, Tahoua, Tillabéri, and Zinder. Heading each department is a prefect, who has a subprefect and a cabinet of advisors.

Departments are further divided into thirty-six sections called *arrondissements*. (This is the French term for the same type of region in France.) Larger communities are officially called towns. In more sparsely populated areas, administrative posts oversee government business.

Sultans and Chiefs

Far more interesting and diverse than official government leaders are Niger's traditional chiefs. Among various ethnic groups, the people look to their traditional nobility as an authority. In the Dosso region, for example, the *Djermakoye* is the traditional ruler of the Djerma people who are the majority there. He is also their most important religious leader. There are seven noble Djerma families whose members are eligible to fill this post.

A Hausa traditional chief

Some Tuareg and Hausa regions have sultans, who are both religious and political leaders. Sultans mediate in domestic disputes, property claims, and so on. People come from miles around to see the sultan for advice on marriage, debts, inheritances, and many other matters. A sultan may even deal with murder cases, although he will usually refer such a matter to the police. The police, in turn, have a high regard and respect for sultans.

The sultan lives in a palace, although it's not the glistening type we might imagine. It may simply be a large residence built in the local style. But compared to regular citizens' houses, it truly is a palace.

The sultan of Zinder with his councillors

Some palaces have a large courtyard where people wait to be called in. Practically anyone may have an audience with the sultan. They need only make an appointment—and then wait their turn. Even for a foreigner, meeting the sultan can be an awesome experience. He wears his traditional long, flowing robes and carries himself with a great sense of dignity.

The most powerful sultans in eastern Niger are the sultan of Zinder and the sultan of Agadez. Maradi also has a well-respected sultan. The sultan of Zinder is a Muslim of the Kanouri ethnic group. His three-story palace is next to Zinder's Grand Mosque.

The sultan of Agadez, or sultan of the Aïr, is the historic ruler of the region's Tuaregs. He is highly respected, and people line up in his courtyard to see him. It used to be the sultan's task to protect the salt caravans (called the *azalai*) across the Ténéré Desert from ambushes by bandits. Now that the salt trade has diminished, he still regulates the caravans and sends escorts with them for protection.

In far eastern Niger, traditional Fulani chiefs have been threatened with removal because they hold so much authority among their people. As for the nomadic Wodaabe, they have great respect for their *Ardo*, or clan chief, and seek his advice. But neither he nor the government has any great political authority over these self-directed cattle herders. They follow the dictates of their ancient cultural traditions.

green trees and grass everywhere, it's hard to believe the Sahara is so near. Niamey receives about 22 inches (56 cm) of rain each year and has an average daily temperature of 84°F (29°C).

The Niger River runs along the west edge of the city. Its main crossing point is the Kennedy Bridge. Near the bridge, modern hotels and high-rise office buildings overlook the river. The bridge continues as the Rue de Kalley, Niamey's major commercial street.

Rue de Kalley ends in a "T" at the Boulevard de la Liberté, the major north-south street. The two meet at the *Grand Marché* (Grand Market), which offers arts and crafts and household goods from all over Africa.

The National Museum and Zoo is an open-air museum covering many acres downtown. Government buildings are modern, yet they are truly African in style. These low-rise, earth-colored structures blend in beautifully with their surroundings. Foreign embassies and the Presidential Palace are on the north side of town, and Niamey's Grand Mosque in on the east side.

Niamey: Did You Know This?

Niamey is one of Africa's most exotic capital cities. Cars and Land Rovers share the byways with camels and donkeys carrying bundles of firewood and piles of straw mats. Modern, high-rise office buildings on well-lighted streets stand in stark contrast to mud homes along dark dirt roads with goats wandering free.

The population—about 400,000 people—is colorful and diverse. Walking down any busy city street are Hausa and Djerma people, Tuaregs swathed in dark-indigo headgear, and Fulani in their pointed hats. In the rainy season, with lush

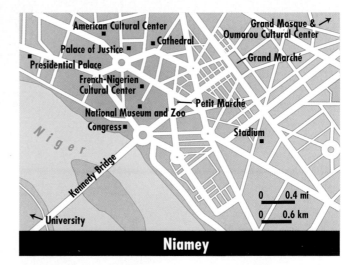

Making a Living

NIGER IS A DESPERATELY POOR COUNTRY. OF THE 174 countries that the United Nations lists according to their economic and social conditions, Niger is number 173. (Only Sierra Leone, also in West Africa, ranks lower.) Almost two-thirds of the people live below Niger's own standard for the poverty level.

In this nation of more than 10 million people, only about 70,000 Nigeriens hold "regular" jobs in the Western sense—that is, jobs that pay wages or salaries. Many others live on the crops and livestock they raise. They may sell or barter their goods for items they can't produce themselves.

Some merchants sell objects they make by hand. Niger's many gifted artisans make mats, baskets, pottery, furniture, farm tools, leather goods, and jewelry. A few enterprising merchants have become wealthy buying and selling goods from Nigeria, Mali, and other countries in the region.

This woman works for an international aid project.

Common Currency

From a money standpoint, it's convenient to travel through West Africa. Travelers don't have to change currencies at every border crossing. The same coins and bills are used in all the countries that belong to the West African Economic and Monetary Union: Benin, Burkina Faso, Ivory Coast, Mali, Niger, Senegal, and Togo. Their basic unit of money is the CFA franc. (CFA stands for *Communauté Financière Africaine,* "African Financial Community.")

CFA banknotes come in denominations of 500, 1,000, 2,500, 5,000, and 10,000 CFA. Coins are issued in 1, 5, 10, 25, 50, 100, and 250 CFA. The 1 CFA coin is rarely used because its value is so small.

Artwork on various CFA banknotes depicts distinguished West Africans, traditional artifacts, village markets, farm activities, and industrial sites such as a mine or a dam on the Niger River.

Cowrie shells from the Indian Ocean were once a form of money throughout much of Africa. Now the Hausa use the word *dala*—their word for cowries—for the 5 CFA coin. Prices in a Nigerien marketplace are sometimes given in terms of dala. For instance, 100 dala equal 500 CFA.

Seasonal migration is a way of life for many Nigeriens. Some villagers have city jobs, for instance, but go back to their rural villages at harvest time. After the harvest, they return to the city to take jobs as laborers and send money back home.

Government Workers

About 43,000 Nigeriens are civil servants; that is, they hold government jobs. They include schoolteachers, hospital workers, the police and military, miners, cement workers, and employees of national radio, television, and newspaper agencies. Niger is gradually trying to privatize its industries—move them from government ownership to private ownership.

A radio station in the city of Zinder

Unpaid wages are a chronic problem among Niger's civil servants. Workers have gone for weeks and even months without pay. Civil servants are organized into trade unions that try to improve their members' working conditions. They have often called industry-wide or nationwide labor strikes to protest overdue wages.

Manufacturing and Trade

Nigerien manufacturing companies produce cement, bricks, textiles, chemicals, soaps, perfumes, and food products.

Hide tanning is one of Niger's industries.

Maradi is known as the economic capital of Niger. It lies in the heart of the farming belt and has hide tanning, food processing, cotton ginning, and other industries. A major road to Nigeria runs out of Maradi, too.

Tillabéri processes sugar and rice, and Niamey makes plastics, paint, chemicals, soft drinks, and leather. Birnin-Konni is a cement-making center. Zinder processes grains, hides, and peanuts and also makes wool blankets and soft drinks.

Some of Niger's top exports are uranium, livestock, cloth, and food. Imports include gasoline and manufactured goods. Nigeria and the Ivory Coast are Niger's main regional trading partners, while France is its major partner outside of Africa.

Most ordinary Nigeriens can't afford to buy more than their basic necessities. Because so few people can count on a steady income, the "black market" trade flourishes in Niger—especially in the south. Gasoline, electrical appliances, cloth, food, and many other items are smuggled from Nigeria and sold on the streets. Government billboards warn citizens that smuggled goods may be inferior or even harmful. Still, selling goods on the black market is a workable way for many Nigeriens to make ends meet.

Eking Out a Living from the Land

"Guinea fowls are our savings bank," says a rural farmer outside of Niamey. He raises guinea fowls in cages that he makes out of branches. In one day he will sell three dozen of these tasty, nutritious birds to merchants in the market. With the proceeds, he plans to buy a sheep for the Tabaski feast and a skirt for his wife.

Raising guinea fowls is just one of the ways Nigerien farmers devise to make a living on their sparse resources. Only about 3 percent of Niger's land can be cultivated, and 7 percent is permanent pastureland. But 90 percent of the people live as farmers or herders.

Crop farmers raise millet, sorghum, rice, corn, and cassava (tapioca) for their own consumption. In small vegetable gardens

next to their homes, they raise tomatoes, carrots, lettuce, okra, and potatoes. Groundnuts (peanuts), cotton, onions, and cowpeas (black-eyed peas) are grown to eat, to sell in the markets, and for export. Cowpeas are Niger's most important export crop. They're called *niébé*. Niger is also a major exporter of onions.

Planting starts in late May or early June, after the first rains. If the summer rains are too heavy, farmers may have to plant a second time. Even then, flooding may wipe out their plantings. Crops also fall victim to grasshoppers, desert locusts, grain-eating birds, and rodents.

A herd of long-horned Zebu cattle

For both nomads and settled farmers, goats and sheep provide milk and meat. Even in the cities, there are goats grazing along the roadsides or milling around in the streets. Niger's nomadic herders count their wealth by the number of animals in their herds. The Tuareg herd camels, while the Wodaabe raise long-horned Zebu cattle. Droughts in the 1970s and 1980s were devastating for these people, wiping out many families' entire herds.

What Niger Grows, Makes, and Mines	
Agriculture (1996)	
Millet	1,832,000 metric tons
Cowpeas	430,000 metric tons
Sorghum	425,000 metric tons
Manufacturing (1993; *value added in CFA francs*)	
Traditional handicrafts	36,900,000,000
Food and beverages	2,900,000,000
Soaps and other chemical products	2,100,000,000
Mining	
Uranium	3,326 metric tons (1996)
Salt	3,000 metric tons (1994)

Mining

Niger contains vast deposits of uranium. It's one of the top uranium producers in the world. The country's economy depends on uranium more than any other resource. In fact, uranium accounts for about half of Niger's export dollars.

In the 1970s, when uranium prices around the world were sky-high, Niger was rolling in money. The government had plenty to spend on government buildings, roads, and social programs. One bad side of this wealth was that prices rose by about 25 percent all over the country. When world prices for uranium dropped in the 1980s, the nation's economy took a nosedive. It has never quite recovered.

Arlit is the main uranium mining center. Uranium is also mined at Akouta, site of the world's largest underground uranium mine. The French began mining operations in Arlit in 1971. Today, Arlit's uranium extracting business is jointly owned by

An aerial view of the uranium mines at Arlit

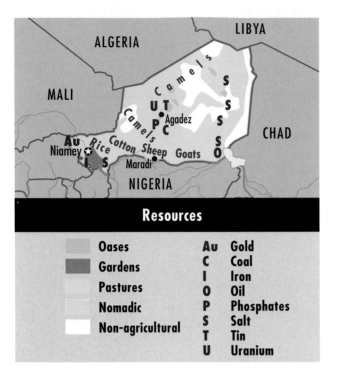

Resources

Oases	Au	Gold
Gardens	C	Coal
Pastures	I	Iron
Nomadic	O	Oil
Non-agricultural	P	Phosphates
	S	Salt
	T	Tin
	U	Uranium

the Nigerien government and a French company. Nigeriens would like to control their own uranium industry, but for now they must depend on the French.

International oil companies are now exploring for oil in eastern Niger. Oil fields have already been discovered nearby in neighboring Chad. Some of Niger's other mineral resources are coal, gold, copper, phosphates, iron ore, tin, tungsten, gypsum, molybdenum, and manganese. But the country's oldest commercial mineral is salt.

The Trans-Saharan Trade

The Saharan trade network first became a big business in around the tenth century, under the Ghana Empire. Islamic Arab merchants, who had spread across North Africa, began running trade caravans between Ghana and the salt-rich desert regions. They traded salt for gold, as well as metal ornaments, leather goods, and cotton cloth. Under the Mali Empire of the 1300s, a second gold–salt trade route went east across the Sahara all the way to Egypt.

The Arab merchants brought more than trade goods. They also brought the religion of Islam; its holy book, the Koran; and the Arabic writing system. In the process, many West African kings and merchants converted to Islam. For some, it was simply "good business"—a way to stay on good terms with traders who brought them so much wealth. As fellow Muslims, they fit in among foreigners. They were also safe from slavery, because no Muslim could enslave another.

Trade across the Sahara reached a peak in the 1400s under Sonni Ali Ber of the Songhai Empire. Arab merchants expanded their trade network from the Atlantic Ocean on the west to Arabia in the east.

Bilma and the Salt Trade

Agadez and the salt-rich oasis of Bilma were important stops on the trans-Saharan trade routes. But, apart from the international trade, these cities had their own regional salt industry.

Pillars of Salt

Standing knee-deep in water, the salt workers of Bilma hack away chunks of salt crusted on the steep banks of a salt pit. They pound the chunks into a powder, then press the salt crystals into pillar-shaped molds. Next they dump the salt pillars out to dry and harden in the sun.

When the Tuareg caravaneers arrive, they negotiate a price per pillar. Times are hard all around, and the price is often lower than the salt merchants would like. Nor can the Tuareg buy as much salt as they once could. Unsold pillars of salt stand for months waiting for buyers.

Nevertheless, a deal is struck—somewhere between 55¢ and 65¢ a pillar. The Tuareg wrap the heavy salt pillars in straw mats or burlap (photo), tie them with rope, and load them onto their camels, tying them down securely. One salt pillar weighs about 50 pounds (23 kg), and each camel can carry eight pillars—four on each side. Once the caravaneers reach Nigeria, they can barter the pillars for as much as four or five times what they paid for them.

Tuareg tribesmen were the kings of the *azalai*, or salt trade. Their camel caravans set out from Agadez for the long trek to Bilma, often stopping in the Fachi salt oasis on the way. After loading up the camels with salt, it was a good forty days' travel to Kano and other cities of Hausaland. There the Tuareg traded salt for millet and other necessities that were scarce in the desert.

Today the salt trade is just about all that's left of the great Saharan caravans. The Tuareg still drive their camels over the same ancient routes—Agadez to Fachi and Bilma, then on to Nigeria or back to Agadez.

Different salt regions produce different grades of salt. The salt from Bilma, for instance, is clean, fine-grained, and good for people to eat. Other regions yield a lower grade of salt suitable for animals.

Old Routes, New Riders

Rusted-out skeletons of cars and trucks are part of the scenery along Niger's desert routes, and even along the main highways. Each skeleton could tell a tale of distress, danger, or death.

On the old desert caravan routes, camels have been replaced by cars, huge cargo trucks, and four-wheel-drive desert vehicles. They go north to Algeria, south to Nigeria, and east from Agadez. Buoys mark the way in some regions, just as they would in the sea.

The safest way to cross the desert is to travel in convoys, or groups, as the camel caravans did. Voyagers in the Sahara must respect the desert. If drivers become careless and lose sight of the other vehicles, it can cost them their lives.

Some drivers let air out of their tires so they can get a better grip on the sand. When wheels do get buried in the soft sand, everyone pitches in to dig them out, sometimes using sheets of metal as ramps.

Getting Around

Riding camels and donkeys—and walking—are still the most common ways to get around in small towns, the rural countryside, and the desert. Farmers load up donkeys or donkey carts to bring their goods to market. Nomads pack all their household possessions onto donkeys when they move to new grazing grounds. Few ordinary Nigeriens can afford to buy cars. Even in Niamey, the traffic seems light for a national capital.

Transporting sorghum by donkey cart

Riding in a vehicle on a paved road has its obstacles. Cattle, sheep, goats, and carts use the roads, too. And checkpoints with roadblocks stop traffic on the way into many of the towns. Armed police or soldiers check everyone's identification papers. Unless the driver slips them a friendly bribe, the travelers might be detained for hours.

Roads and Airports

Niger developed its highway system under French colonial rule and expanded it with income from uranium. The road to Arlit is called the "uranium highway." It was built during Niger's uranium boom in the 1970s.

Today Niger has about 6,275 miles (10,100 km) of roads, and less than one-tenth of that mileage is paved. Even on paved roads, travel can be slow. Speed bumps slow drivers down on the way into villages. So do the police, when they stop and check the papers of anyone driving through.

Traveling by truck on one of Niger's few paved roads

One paved highway runs all the way across southern Niger. North-south highways duplicate the old caravan routes out of Hausaland, whose major cities were in Nigeria. The highway through Birnin-Konni runs south to Sokoto (Nigeria) and north through Tahoua to Agadez. From Maradi, it's a short drive south to Katsina and on to Kano. Zinder was a great crossroads for trade in the old days. From Zinder, a highway now runs south to Kano and north to Agadez.

While it's easy to travel between the bigger cities, most roads in Niger are unpaved. A few have gravel surfaces, but many consist only of tracks or furrows left in the dirt or sand by other drivers. They often wash out during the rainy season.

Niger has no railways. There are about twenty-seven airports, and fewer than half of them have paved runways. Diori International Airport in Niamey handles flights to and from other African countries and Europe.

Spreading the Word

Freedom of the press in Niger has often depended on who is in power. Under non-democratic regimes, news reports have been limited to the "official" versions of events. Journalists with other views have been harassed, held for questioning, or even imprisoned. Niger's return to a democratic government in 1999 was good news for local journalists.

All of Niger's newspapers are published in Niamey. *Le Sahel*, the national news agency's daily paper, has the largest circulation. *L'Alternative*, *Anfani*, and *Le Républicain* are the other major newspapers. All three are published weekly.

Le Sahel **is the best-selling newspaper in Niger.**

It's an odd surprise to see satellite dishes rising over the countryside. But even before satellite service arrived, some rural communities had solar-powered cable television. People would gather around the neighborhood TV set to watch shows from the United States.

Niger has one television network with about eighteen stations, as well as about two dozen radio stations. The government controls Niger's TV and radio systems. Télé Sahel is the national television service. La Voix du Sahel, the national radio service, broadcasts in French, Hausa, Djerma, and several other local languages.

CHAPTER

SEVEN

People of Many Cultures

T HE PEOPLE OF NIGER ARE TYPICALLY FRIENDLY, CONSIDerate, and tolerant of others. Men, women, and children—young and old alike—smile and wave to strangers passing through the countryside. Nigeriens also have a strong sense of tradition and family loyalty. Even though so many of them are very poor, they have a deep sense of "belonging" and take pride in who they are.

Niger is home to about 10.1 million people, according to the United Nations' 1999 estimates. That figure is expected to more than double by the year 2025 and triple by 2050.

Such rapid growth is surprising in a country where illness and disease take a heavy toll. Out of every 1,000 babies born in Niger, close to 300 die before reaching the age of five.

In spite of the high rate of child deaths, Nigerien families are large. The average Nigerien woman bears seven children in her lifetime. Today, almost half the population is under fifteen years of age. As these young people become parents themselves, the population will skyrocket.

Opposite: **Hausa woman**

Population distribution in Niger

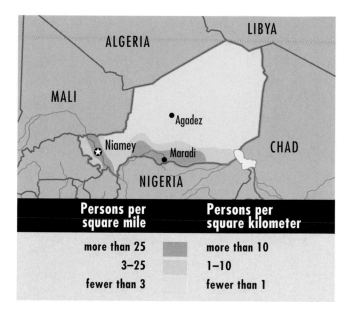

On average, a Nigerien can expect to live only forty-seven years. Sadly, both adults and children die of diseases that are easily prevented or cured. One is malaria. It causes about 10 percent of all deaths throughout Africa and 25 percent of children's deaths. The mosquitoes that cause malaria breed in stagnant water and open sewers.

Meningitis is another deadly disease. Over 4,000 Nigeriens—an all-time high—died of meningitis in 1995. Measles, polio, tuberculosis, and malnutrition are other common causes of death.

Where People Live

About 90 percent of all Nigeriens live within 100 miles (161 km) of the southern border. Most people live in the rural countryside as settled farmers or as nomadic or semi-nomadic herders. More than 75 percent of Nigeriens are farmers who live on the crops and animals they raise.

Niamey, the capital, is Niger's largest city. Zinder and Maradi, the second- and third-largest cities, are both in the far south, near the border of Nigeria. Next in size are Tahoua, in south-central Niger, and Agadez, in the north.

Remnants of Ancient Empires

Niger is a place where many different ethnic groups have lived together for thousands of years. Foreigners crossed paths in Niger because the territory was crisscrossed with trade caravans from distant lands. Cultures overlapped there, too, as Niger stood on the fringes of several great African empires.

Hausa people make up about 56 percent of Niger's population—more than 5 million people. They make their living as farmers, traders, and leather and textile craftsmen. Their traditional role as merchants is still very much alive, too. Some of the most successful merchants in Agadez and in southern Niger are Hausa.

Hausa people live throughout the country, but most make their homes in south-central Niger. This region is the northern edge of historical Hausaland. Nigeria, just across the border, is the Hausa heartland, where over 20 million Hausa live.

A Hausa boy in Agadez

The Songhai-Djerma make up about 22 percent of the population. They're descendants of warriors and administrators of the illustrious Songhai Empire. The Djerma are an ethnic subgroup of the Songhai, but the two groups are usually considered one people.

Who Lives in Niger?

Hausa	56%
Songhai-Djerma	22%
Fulani	8.5%
Tuareg	8%
Kanouri-Manga	4.3%
Arab, French, others	1.2%

Djerma girls on their way home from school

Today the Djerma live throughout much of southwest Niger. Most are farmers, and their traditional homes are round houses made of straw. The Songhai who live along the banks of the Niger River are fishermen and rice growers.

Djerma people make up the majority of the population in the Niamey and Dosso areas. Because the French first set up schools in Niamey, the Djerma were among the first Nigeriens to receive a formal education. As a result, they had a strong influence in the new government after independence. Many Djerma still hold posts as government officials and civil servants.

The Noble and the Free

Nomadic Tuareg in the desert

Once-powerful masters of the Saharan salt trade, the Tuareg now make up about 8 percent of Niger's population. They are descended from the North African Berbers, and Niger's northern mountains and desert are still their domain.

Tuareg, in Arabic, means "forsaken by God." Arabs who brought Islam to North Africa found them hard to convert. But in their own language of Tamasheq, the Tuareg call themselves *Imashaghen*, or *Imohagh*, meaning "the noble and the free." Outsiders call the Tuareg the Blue Men of the Desert because the indigo dye of their clothing comes off on their skin, leaving a deep-blue tint.

Dark-skinned Tuareg girls

Because of their Caucasian ancestry, full-blooded Tuareg people have light skin, straight or wavy hair, and blue or grey eyes. Through marriages with other ethnic groups, many Tuareg have darker skin and eyes and curlier hair.

Tuareg warriors fiercely resisted French colonial rule through one revolt after another. To a great extent, the French broke down their social order. Tensions are still alive in Niger today as the Tuareg struggle for self-determination, equal opportunities, and equal representation in government. They are intent on preserving *tamoust*—a word that encompasses their traditional culture, outlook, and ways of life.

The Fulani make up about 8.5 percent of the population. Also known as Peul, Fula, or Fulbe, they may have migrated from the Upper Nile River region many centuries ago. Historically, the Fulani were nomadic cattle herders, but over time, most settled down. Most of Niger's Fulani live in south-central Niger, where they farm and raise livestock. Fulani merchants in their traditional pointed hats can be seen in market towns throughout the country.

One group of Fulani—the Wodaabe, or Bororo Fulani—have kept to their traditional nomadic life. Their lives revolve around their herds, and they still migrate across the Sahel region seeking fresh grazing grounds.

A tattooed Fulani woman

The name *Wodaabe* means "people of the taboo." This means that they are set apart from the others, clinging to ancient Fulani codes of behavior and modesty. Of all Nigeriens, the Wodaabe are the most independent and separate from modern life.

The Wodaabe are famous for their "beauty pageants." In this annual series of dances, the men make themselves beautiful with alluring makeup and spectacular adornments. Then they dance for the women, each man hoping to be named the most beautiful or to attract a new wife.

Other Minorities

The Kanouri live in the southeast, between Zinder and Lake Chad. They make up about 4.3 percent of the population.

A Kanouri girl

They are people of mixed origins, with ancestors from half a dozen ethnic groups. Salt processing is one of the Kanouris' main occupations, along with farming, fishing, and livestock raising.

Niger is also home to small numbers of other ethnic groups. The Bella, former slaves of the Tuareg, are now farmers living near Tuareg settlements. The

Toubou, who originated in Chad, live in the Lake Chad region. Near the Burkina Faso border are the Mossi and the Gourmantché. Arabs live in the north and far eastern parts of the country, and about 1,200 French people live in their former colony.

Speaking in Many Tongues

Crowds of children gather around any foreigner who strolls into a town or marketplace. All it takes to become instant friends is to say "*ça va?*" (French for "How's it going?"). "*Ça va bien*" ("It's going fine") is the reply.

Many Nigeriens—even the children—speak two or more languages. French became Niger's official language during the

This billboard in French is about family planning.

Common Phrases (pronunciations only)

French

How's it going?	sa VAH
(response)	sa vah bee-EHN
Thank you.	mer-SEE
Good-bye.	oh ruh-VWAR

Hausa

Hello.	sah-NOO
(response)	YAH-wah sah-NOO
How are you?	BAR-kah
I'm fine.	LAH-fee-ah LO
Thank you.	na-GO-day

Djerma

Good morning.	ma-teen-keh-NEE
How are you?	BAR-kah
Thank you.	fo-fo
Good-bye.	ka-LAH ton-ton

Tamasheq

How do you do?	met-al-ee-kah
I'm fine.	eel-ka-rahs
Thank you.	tan-oo-mert
Good-bye.	harr-sad

Fulfulde

Hello.	FOH-mah
How's it going?	ah-DYAH-mo
It's going fine.	sah-GO
I'm happy to be here.	may-NAH-nee bell-DOON

French colonial days. Today, French is spoken across the country—in social life and marketplaces, as well as in government and professional activities.

Unofficially, though, Hausa is Niger's major language. It's much more widely spoken than French. In fact, about 80 percent of Nigeriens can speak Hausa. Historically, the Hausa were expert merchants and administrators. As they spread into cities and towns of Niger, Hausa became the common language for business and trade. Hausa is typically written with Arabic characters.

Because Hausa trade networks spread so widely, Hausa is one of the most important languages in all of West Africa. An estimated 40 million people speak Hausa as either their first or second language. In Nigeria, it's the primary language. Hausa speakers also live in Cameroon, Togo, Burkina Faso, Benin, and Ghana. Even beyond West Africa, there are people who speak Hausa in Chad, the Sudan, and the Congo.

Djerma (sometimes spelled Zerma) is another familiar language in Niger. Djerma speakers are especially common in the southwest, where Songhai and Djerma people kept their loyalty to the fallen Songhai Empire. Djerma and Songhai are actually related dialects, widely understood on both sides. Knowing a few basic greetings and phrases in Djerma can be very useful in the markets of Niamey and other riverside towns.

Tamasheq is the ancient language of the Tuareg. It's written in a script called *tifinar*. The Fulani speak Fulfulde, and the Kanouri speak Kanouri. Arabic dialects are spoken around Agadez and in the far north and east. Many Nigeriens also speak English fairly well. In the secondary schools, it's a required language.

A Tuareg boy learning to write in the tifinar script

Spiritual Lives

RELIGION IS A CENTRAL FORCE IN NIGERIENS' EVERYDAY lives. Ancient religious traditions still have a strong foothold, even among people who consider themselves Muslims or Christians. Most of these traditional beliefs are a form of animism—a reverence for spirits in animals, plants, and other manifestations of nature.

The great majority of Nigeriens are Muslims, or followers of Islam. Estimates of Niger's Muslim presence range from 85 to 95 percent of the population. Christianity has made only small inroads into Niger, with less than 0.5 percent of the population.

Opposite: **Muslims observing their noon prayers at a market in Niamey**

Religions of Niger

Islam	88.7%
Animism	11%
Christianity	0.3%

Reading the Koran, the Islamic holy book

The Ways of Islam

A Tuareg holy man teaching the Koran to a group of children

Islam is the religion of the entire Arab world. It reached Niger via Arab trade routes through West Africa. Muslims believe in one god, and his name is Allah. His prophet, Muhammad, began teaching Islam in the Arabian city of Mecca in the seventh century A.D. Through trade and military conquest, Islam quickly spread from Arabia through the Middle East and much of Africa.

Muhammad's teachings are written in the Koran, the Islamic book of holy scriptures. Islamic law covers every aspect of daily life, from food and clothing to education, manners, and how to carry on business. Besides being a spiritual text, the Koran has been a powerful educational tool. By studying the Koran, people throughout the Islamic world have learned to read and write Arabic. This is still true today.

A devout Muslim observes the Five Pillars of Islam. They are: belief in Allah as the one god and in Muhammad as his prophet; praying five times a day, facing the holy city of Mecca; giving alms to the poor; fasting during the holy month of Ramadan; and making a pilgrimage (*hajj*) to Mecca at least once.

Islam allows polygamy, the practice of having more than one wife. A Muslim man may take another wife when he feels he can afford the added expense. Four wives is the customary limit. Naturally, wives are sometimes jealous of one another. But quite often, they get along like sisters, pleasantly sharing their chores. The first wife is always regarded with special courtesy.

Most towns and villages have a *marabout* (MARE-a-boo). He is an Islamic priest, teacher, and advisor on spiritual matters. People consult the marabout about the proper way to handle family, community, or business matters. The marabout also trains boys in the teachings of the Koran and in Arabic writing.

Many Muslims, especially among Arabs and Tuaregs, believe in *jinni*. According to Islamic legend, the jinni are spirits that can take on human or animal form. The English word *genie* is derived from jinni.

An Islamic reform movement called *Izala* has recently spread to Niger from neighboring Nigeria. Izala aims to cleanse Western influences from Nigerien society. Adherents insist, for example, that women follow the Islamic tradition of wearing veils in public.

Usman dan Fodio (1754-1817), also called the Shaykh, was a Fulani religious and political leader. Born in the Hausa state of Gobir (now in northwest Nigeria), he became the most important West African religious reformer of his time. A serious Muslim student, he was initiated into Islam's mystical Sufi order. As a teacher, he gained a wide following among the Fulani and Hausa peoples. In time, more and more communities looked to him as a religious and political leader. Usman waged *jihad* (holy war) against the caliph of Gobir and defeated him in 1808. Then he established his own caliphate (Islamic domain) at Sokoto, where he continued to teach until he died. Usman left behind an enormous amount of writings in both Arabic and Fulfulde.

Mosques

The mosque is the traditional Islamic house of worship. The faithful remove their shoes before entering. Inside, men kneel upon mats as they pray. The minaret is a high tower near the mosque from which the *muezzin* calls Muslims to their daily prayers.

This mosque in Agadez was built in the traditional West African style in the sixteenth century.

Two very different styles of mosques are seen in Niger. Those in traditional West African style are earth-colored structures surrounded by a wall. Like many local homes and public buildings, they're built of sun-dried earth. Their tall, rocket-shaped minarets bristle with protruding wooden beams.

The other style resembles mosques in Middle Eastern countries. They are often

A Middle Eastern style mosque in Niamey

white with blue, green, or gold ornamentation and topped with a dome. Muslims from Saudi Arabia, Egypt, and other Islamic nations provided the funds to build them. The Grand Mosque in Niamey, for example, was financed by Libya.

Ancient Beliefs

Traditional beliefs are still strong among people in Niger's rural communities. Pleading for rain is the point of many rituals. Some people believe that rain does not come because the gods need blood. That need is met by slaughtering a sheep on the gravesite of an ancestor. Others believe that God takes pity on a poor, hot creature—such as a toad—and therefore sends rain.

Some families believe in totems—animals that protect them from harm. A family or household has its own protective totem, which could be a certain dog or cat, or a wild animal such as a bird or snake. The totem is always treated kindly, just as if it were a member of the family. Another protector is the *toru*, a household god who watches over everyone in the home.

Other beliefs center around witches and sorcery. A witch is a man or woman who can change into any form at all—an animal, or even the wind. Wearing an amulet around the neck

The Day of the Toad

The earth was parched, and the millet was dying. Amadou's mother told him to fetch a toad. He found one in a cool, shady spot and brought it to her. She tied a string around its leg, then filled a large calabash (bowl) with water.

Balancing the calabash on her head, she walked to the village center, while Amadou followed with the toad. Women and children gathered around as she placed the calabash on the ground with a smaller bowl floating inside. Near the calabash, she drove a stick into the ground and tied the string with the toad to it.

Amadou's mother began to beat out a rhythm on the bowl. Old women sat close by and began to sing prayers for rain. Amadou and the others circled round and round them, answering each prayer with "So be it!"

On and on they went as the day wore on. The sun beat down upon their heads, and the toad hopped about on his string. In mid-afternoon, dark clouds began to gather. By sundown, great torrents of rain were pouring from the sky.

Even now, after getting his university degree, Amadou does not know what to make of this incident.

or waist can help keep these evil spirits away. Children are not allowed to roam around after sunset, for that's when witches are on the prowl.

It's believed that the witch can catch a person's soul and cast a spell on it, or even change it into an animal. That person gets very sick. A medicine man concocts a remedy and says prayers to drive off the spell. In case of a spirit possession, the *bori*—a sorcerer or medium—goes into a trance and lets spirits enter his body as part of the exorcism ritual.

Islam is the religion of most Djerma people, and they observe Islamic prayer and fasting practices. But their faith is mixed with animism, the belief that spirits inhabit many things around them. Various spirit cults involve spirit possession and magic. Cult priests are believed to be able to take on a spirit's powers, drive out possessions, and heal.

Among the Hausa, there is a small minority of non-Muslims, or "pagans." In the Maradi region they are called *Maguzawa*, and in the Dogondoutchi area they are the *yan kasa* (sons of the earth). They follow the traditional Hausa religion, which has a variety of good and evil spirits. Family and clan ancestors are honored at log shrines, where sacrifices are made in times of trouble. Holy men conduct various rituals and initiate young men into adulthood within a sacred grove of trees. The priests also diagnose the spiritual reason for illnesses, prescribe cures, and perform exorcisms.

Important Religious Holidays

Tabaski *(Id al-Adha* or *Id al-Kebir)*	Date varies
Islamic New Year	Date varies
Id al-Moulid (Muhammad's birthday)	Date varies
Ramadan begins	Date varies
Id al-Fitr (end of Ramadan)	Date varies
Christmas	December 25

Islam did not wipe out African traditions. Instead, Islamic beliefs became woven into the fabric of people's existing lives. Islamic culture and traditions also found their way into native African political and social life and arts.

Ancient Songhai beliefs are rooted in ancestor worship. When an ancestor is present in a certain place, the ancestor is believed to protect that place and everyone near it from evil. The markers for these holy places are conical earthen or stone pillars. When Islam arrived, the Songhai built the minarets of their mosques in the form of these pillars.

The *malam* is an Islamic teacher, scholar, or healer. His healing role is very much like that of Niger's traditional, non-Muslim healers. The malam listens to a patient's complaint. Then he searches the Koran for a passage that fits the illness and writes the verse on a piece of wood. The patient takes the wood home, washes the writing off in a bowl of water, and drinks the water. As one malam explains, "Allah is in the medicine."

Although the Tuareg are Muslims, they follow Islam in their own way. They honor most Muslim holidays but do not observe Ramadan, the month of fasting. A Tuareg man wears amulets that contain verses of the Koran and other magical inscriptions. This assures protection for himself and his camel herds.

Even when they have a college education, wealth, and a modern lifestyle, many Nigeriens are quite comfortable with their ancestors' traditions. They may request the services of a spirit medium or traditional healer, even spending large sums

for protection from the evil eye and other forms of sorcery. Such evils could cost them their jobs or their health. Thus, the old traditions are adapted to modern-day needs.

Tuareg women and children praying

Expressing the Culture

MOST AFRICAN ART HAS BOTH A PRACTICAL USE AND a social or spiritual meaning. A big marketplace, with rows and rows of artisans' stalls, is not just a shopping center for pretty things. Local shoppers may be looking for an amulet to ward off evil, a wedding blanket for a daughter, beads to wear in a village ritual, or a wood carving to represent a child who has died.

Opposite: **Clay pots for sale in an open-air market**

Vendors offering vegetables for sale in a bustling market

Marketplaces

Niger's open-air markets are hectic jumbles of people and their goods. Booths are piled high with rugs and mattresses or crammed with textiles, leather goods, and jewelry. Spices, vegetables, and grain are spread out on mats on the ground. Donkeys, camels, sheep, and goats stand waiting to be sold.

Nothing in the outdoor markets has a convenient price tag. Bargaining is the way business is done. A merchant names a price that's as much as twice the object's worth. Through a friendly ritual of shock and giving in, buyer and seller reach an agreement.

On Sunday mornings, the Niger River becomes a busy highway for people coming to the market at Ayorou. As they paddle up in their long boats, they weave their way around hippos bobbing in the river. This is one of West Africa's largest markets for cattle, camels, donkeys, sheep, and goats. There's also a dazzling array of spices, vegetables, calabashes (gourd bowls), clothing, and silver and leather goods. Even more colorful than the market goods are the people. People from dozens of regional ethnic groups arrive, each dressed in traditional robes, headdresses, and jewelry.

In Niamey, the main supermarket is Score. But shopping in the outdoor markets is much more interesting. Niamey's Grand Marché is a maze of crowded aisles bristling with textiles, clothing, jewelry, and household goods. In the Thieves' Market, or Recycling Market, shoppers can find items such as

Score is the main supermarket in Niamey.

The National Museum

The National Museum of Niger spreads out across 60 acres (24 hectares) of downtown Niamey. It's a cultural and educational museum, a zoo, and an artisans' showplace all in one. Outdoor cages showcase many of Niger's native animals, from lions to ostriches.

One area features traditional dwellings of Niger's main ethnic groups—Hausa, Djerma, Tuareg, Fulani, and Toubou. There are also exhibits of the various groups' traditional clothing, jewelry, weapons, leatherwork, and musical instruments. Separate buildings cover Niger's geology and paleontology. One little enclosure houses the remains of the Tree of the Ténéré, the famous desert landmark.

In the artisans' co-op are craftspeople from every corner of the country, making and selling silver jewelry, leather goods, wood carvings, woven blankets, and decorated textiles.

The artisans are happy to talk about their work and to show visitors how they do it—regardless of any language barriers. Here, and throughout the sprawling museum complex, it's obvious that Nigeriens are proud of their culture and their national identity.

mats, pots, and pans made out of recycled plastic and metal. They can also buy faucets, hub caps, batteries, and foods such as huge cassava roots.

This woman is wearing traditional Tuareg silver jewelry.

Handicrafts

The Tuareg are expert silversmiths. Silver, they believe, is a pure metal favored by Muhammad. Tuareg silversmiths make crosses of many designs, each one an insignia for a region or town. Silver amulets and talismans are made for safety and protection. Tuareg men's traditional rings are silver set with carnelian, a reddish stone. Carnelian is valued for its healing powers, especially for disorders of the blood. The Tuareg were fierce warriors, and so they are expert makers of daggers and swords.

Tuareg Crosses

Among the Tuareg, both men and women wear the famous Tuareg silver crosses. Each confederation has its traditional design, which is named after a region or town. The maker carves his name on the back of the cross. Two of the best-known designs are the Agadez cross and the Iferouane cross. Others are the Tahoua, Zinder, and Kaoule crosses.

Each cross design is rich with meaning. Symbols such as the chameleon's eye and the jackal's tracks represent power and cunning. The four arms of the cross are meant to banish evil to the north, south, east, and west. Traditionally, a Tuareg father presented a cross to his son when he reached puberty. "I give you the four corners of the world," he would say, "because one cannot know where one will die."

Though most of the cross designs are very old, a new one was added recently. It honors the Tuareg rebel leader Mano Dayak, who died in an airplane crash in 1995.

The Djerma weave long, colorful strips that are sewn together to make blankets. Individual strips can be used as wall hangings, too. When the weaver sits at his loom, the long lengthwise threads are anchored by a weight that sits several

A Djerma weaver at work

yards, or meters, ahead of him. The Hausa, too, are weavers. Their blankets are used as wedding presents and remain the woman's property even if a couple divorces.

Nigeriens make beautiful leather purses, saddlebags, saddles, and sandals. Tuareg craftspeople tint the leather with red, green, and black dyes. To create their distinctive leather designs, they lay several layers of leather over one another with carved patterns that let the colors show through. An entire goatskin may end up as one ornately decorated shoulder bag.

Colorful wood carvings

Wood carvers make statues, masks, elephants, antelopes, and chess sets out of mahogany and ebony. These woods are usually imported from elsewhere in West Africa because they are not very abundant in Niger. Metalsmiths make bronze figurines of people and African animals. Bracelets, buckles, and ornamental daggers are often made of bronze, brass, or nickel instead of expensive silver and gold.

Textile artisans produce tie-dyed fabrics and brightly colored batiks of African scenes. Wax cloth—with its crinkly, veined patterns—is actually made in Holland. Blankets include camel-hair covers and Tuareg wedding blankets. Mud cloth, a specialty in Mali, is usually russet-colored with geometric patterns in black. Wodaabe men's black tunics are completely covered with row upon row of colorful embroidery. From the hem hang cowrie shells that click and rattle when the man moves.

Storytelling, Folktales, and Legends

At night under the stars, while sipping hot tea brewed over an open fire, it's only a matter of time before the stories begin to come out. Storytelling is an honored tradition in Niger. Even among adults, telling animal tales is a respected pastime. The usual cast of characters could be hyenas, lions, donkeys, goats, or monkeys. Each animal behaves in a typical way—whether it's lazy, greedy, or crafty—and the tale ends with a moral about human behavior.

For centuries, people passed down the stories of their history from generation to generation. Even now, there are old men in Niger who can recite several hundred years' worth of their clan's history.

Griots are professional storyteller-musicians who relate a village's history and ancestry in song. The griot also teaches, mediates disputes, and plays an important part in village ceremonies. He uses different musical techniques for epic

Cowrie Shells

It may seem odd to see seashells in landlocked Niger. But cowrie shells appear everywhere, from clothing and jewelry to hair ornamentation. Found throughout Africa, the cowries come from the Indian Ocean. People used to use the shells as money. But cowries are also rich with religious symbolism. Among many African peoples, they are symbols of fertility.

The Tale of Samba and Lobo

A Fulani folk tale tells of a courageous young man named Samba who was to marry a beautiful and virtuous girl named Lobo. On their wedding day, the king rode in and took Lobo away to be his own wife. Samba went to the palace one night and crept into the bedroom. He held a knife to the king's throat and sang love songs to Lobo all through the night. The next day, Samba told the story before the elders of the kingdom and proved that the king was a coward. The elders ruled that Samba deserved to have Lobo after all. Thus, by his great cunning and courage, Samba won his beloved Lobo back.

histories, proverbs, singing a great man's praises, and so on. The profession of griot arose under West Africa's thirteenth-century Mali Empire. Traditionally, griots belong to a hereditary social class.

One famous piece of oral literature is the *Kano Chronicle*. It details the history of Hausaland's Kano kingdom. Relying on centuries of oral tradition, it was not written down until the 1890s.

Religious mythology makes for another collection of tales. Good and bad spirits, their family squabbles and histories, their favorite colors and trinkets, what they demand of humans and why—all these subjects can fill hours of story-telling time. Often, it's the grandparents who tell these tales to children. It's a way of passing on the society's culture and values and giving children a sense of who they are.

The Sheltering Sky

Italian film director Bernardo Bertolucci's 1990 movie *The Sheltering Sky* was the first to bring Tuareg culture to the American screen. Starring Debra Winger and John Malkovich, it was based on a novel by Paul Bowles. Tuareg leader Mano Dayak coordinated parts of the movie that were shot in the Sahara Desert, including a long segment in Agadez. Dayak recruited many of his own friends and family members to play the parts of Tuareg people.

Traditional Music

The simplest form of music in Niger is singing to the beat of clapping hands. A hollow calabash or even a metal gasoline can might be used as a drum. Tuareg women beat out rhythms on a simple, homemade type of drum—a large calabash of water with a gourd floating in it. As the woman beats on the gourd, the sound resounds through the water to the outer calabash.

Traditional folk instruments in Niger include two-stringed and three-stringed lutes and many kinds of drums. The *molo* is a traditional Fulani guitar. The *kora* is a harp with twenty-one strings and a calabash as the resonating body. It looks more like a banjo with a long neck than a harp. It was the traditional instrument of griots, and expert kora players still perform today.

The *kalangou* is one of many African drums known as "talking drums." It's a tall wooden cylinder with hides stretched across the ends. Kalangous produce a wide range of pitches, from very high to very low. Because Hausa is a tonal language, a talented kalangou player can "speak" messages of joy or sorrow by imitating language tones (high, low, or falling, for instance) that the audience can recognize.

The *imzad* is a type of violin played only by Tuareg women. Its rounded body is made of wood or a dried calabash gourd

A Tuareg woman playing the imzad

covered with hide. The imzad's one string is hair from a horse's tail, and it's played with a curved-wood bow. Typically, a woman plays the imzad to accompany improvised songs that glorify Tuareg bravery and heroism.

Nigerien dramas are traditional entertainments that remain very popular today. Both city and rural residents enjoy these theater performances—either live or on television.

Sports

African-style wrestling is a popular spectator sport for Nigeriens. Matches are held in Niamey's *Stade de la Lutte Traditionelle* (Stadium for Traditional Wrestling). One match may last as little as a minute or as long as six minutes.

Wrestling opponents use ritual hand movements to distract each other. They also invoke spiritual help to improve their chances of winning. The object of a match is to get both of the opponent's knees on the ground. Then the winner struts around the arena as the cheering crowd tosses money down to him.

Both girls and boys enjoy basketball, volleyball, and soccer (called football in Niger). Niger's university students sometimes

Woaley

Woaley is a game similar to backgammon that originated in ancient Egypt. Today, it's a popular game for both children and adults throughout Africa. A woaley board is a long rectangle, about 18 inches (46 cm) long. It has two rows of cups—one row for each player—with six cups in each row. The game pieces are peas, and forty-eight peas come with the game. The two opponents try to capture each others' peas. Some woaley boards have a cup at each end to hold captured peas.

Onlookers watch as two Tuareg men battle in a mock sword fight.

compete in sports events with students of other West African countries. The games may include basketball and volleyball for both boys and girls, as well as soccer and handball. Martial arts are popular in West Africa, so karate, judo, and tae kwon do matches may round out the events.

Both men's and women's teams compete in the National Basketball Cup tournament every year. Niger has been holding National Cup tournaments for soccer since 1974. There are national wrestling and judo championships, too.

Niger's professional athletes are fierce competitors in international events. Niger competes with neighboring countries for the West African Football Union Cup and takes part in the All Africa Games. Even though Niger is not famous for its beaches, Nigeriens participated in the first African Beach Volleyball Championships held in Casablanca, Morocco, in 1999.

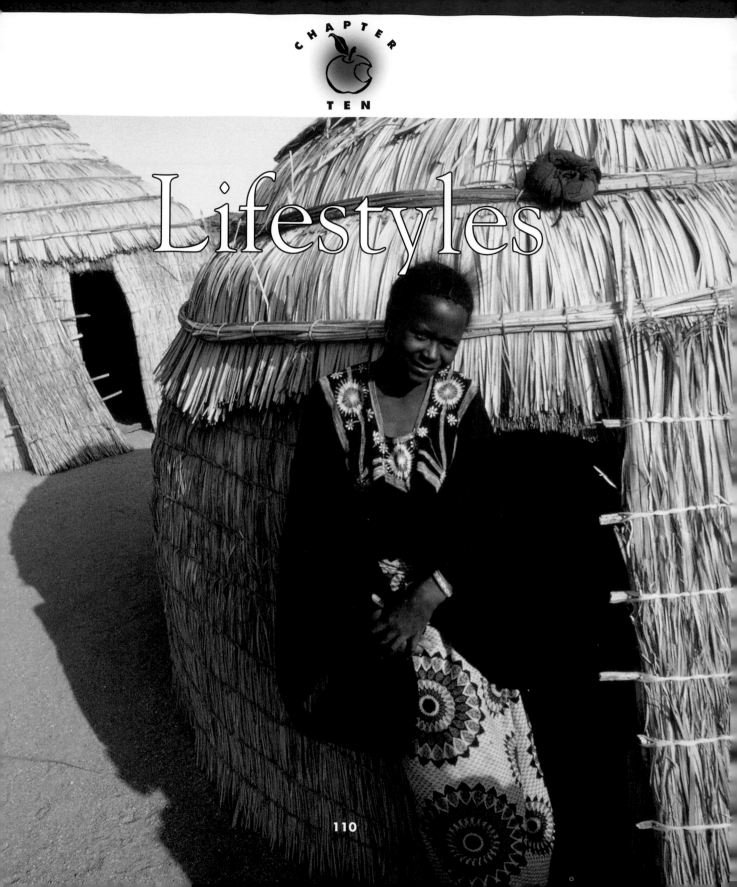

Lifestyles

CITY LIFE AND RURAL LIFE IN NIGER ARE WORLDS apart. Teenagers in Niamey might spend a summer afternoon at the swimming pool. In the evening, they may watch a movie or go dancing in a nightclub. Meanwhile, their village cousins are married with children. Their days are spent cooking, tilling the fields, or herding cattle.

Some young people in rural villages attend public schools. If they pass their college entrance exams, they leave the countryside to get a college education in Niamey. When they come back home for a visit, they often have trouble communicating with older villagers. It's hard to explain events that go on in the city. And they quickly find that scientific facts, health precautions, or modern politics are not welcome subjects. Their elders scold them for losing their spiritual values.

While their lifestyles may differ, city and rural Nigeriens cannot help but share each others' worlds. Even the most traditional villagers are connected to modern ways through television, radio, markets, and travels. They have access to boom boxes, T-shirts, watches, and many other modern goods. Educated city people may visit doctors and pharmacies, but they are also likely to use traditional amulets, herbal medicines, and spirit mediums to ensure good health.

A traffic jam in Niamey

In a rural village, women begin working before the sun is up. They pound millet, fetch water from the village well or pump, gather firewood, feed the animals, and cook. Many women earn their own pocket money with services such as braiding hair or selling prepared food. Usually the women serve meals to the men first and eat later. The husband makes decisions for the family and takes other wives when he feels he is ready.

Women fetching drinking water from a modern pump near Zinder

Young people marry close relatives, especially cousins, when possible. A young man may be in his twenties when he takes his first wife. But for a girl, it's time to get married when she is between twelve and fifteen years old.

Either the girl's father or the village chief decides who her husband will be. A villager may offer his daughter to an aged holy man as a kind of spiritual good work. Even if the girl is in school and making good grades, she is taken out of school to marry. Women can divorce their husbands, however. It's not uncommon for a woman to go through three or four marriages in her lifetime.

The early-marriage system is breaking down, but only in small degrees. Today, few girls marry before age fifteen. Some parents are determined to educate their daughters. And Nigerien women have just begun to demand their rights. But tradition is a strong force among Nigeriens. Changing the role of women could put their traditional societies in turmoil.

Hausa Traditions

In Hausa communities, people live in walled compounds enclosing brick or straw huts. The huts surround a central courtyard. Men have their own huts, while the wives live in separate huts. One compound encloses a family unit—a man and his wives and children, and often the families of his brothers and uncles, too. The oldest man of the extended family is the chief of the compound.

Farmland is divided among a Hausa man's male heirs. With each new generation, there is less land to go around. Men usually rely on other skills to bring in extra income. They may work as tailors, barbers, craftsmen, or merchants to earn cash for food or medicine.

When the rainy season is over and the harvesting is done, some men leave the village and migrate to the city to work. They may be gone six months or more. By laboring during the dry season, they guard against poverty in case of a drought.

Granaries used to store millet

Djerma Traditions

In Djerma villages, houses are typically round with mud walls and a straw-thatched roof. Granaries for storing millet are huge, round, mud-walled structures raised up on stilts to guard against moisture.

Djerma traditions are similar in many ways to Hausa customs. The oldest male is the head of the *windi*, or household. Each wife has her own separate house where she and her children live. Boys take care of the family's farm animals, while girls help pound millet and take care of younger children. Many Djerma men are merchants who travel to markets in other cities and countries. Others are expert potters, basket makers, or weavers.

Near the end of the dry season, the Djerma hold the *yenendi* (cooling-off) ceremony. This is a time for music and dancing and calling on the spirits to bring heavy rains and a bountiful harvest. (The Hausa have a similar ceremony, called *Watam Bakwai*—"seventh month.")

Tuareg Culture

The Tuareg are organized into several confederations named by region. People of the Kel Aïr confederation, for instance, occupy the Aïr region. Within each confederation are family-based clans.

Tuareg society is matrilineal—that is, ancestors and descendants are figured through the line of the mothers, rather than the fathers. The Tuareg also follow a caste system, with various professions and lifestyles assigned to a social class.

Tuareg women enjoy a power and freedom that's unheard-of among women in other Muslim societies. They are not veiled, they can own property, and they keep their social class even if they marry someone of a lower caste. Women can choose their husbands and divorce them, although a Tuareg man cannot divorce his wife.

Life on the Salt Road

Making the trek to the salt pits is not an easy job. The caravaneers rise before dawn and load up their camels with traveling supplies. The camels make a deafening racket, bellowing and roaring all the while. By sunrise, the caravan is underway. Because the camels are loaded with cargo, the men amble alongside them on foot.

No one stops for a midday meal. Instead, they pass around bowls of milk or millet mush as they march along. Once they reach the heart of the Ténéré Desert, the landscape is an endless sea of sand in all directions. But the men know their route by instinct, by the position of the sun, and by an occasional landmark of stone.

At sundown they stop, kneel facing the east, and say their evening prayers. Then they continue on, navigating in the darkness by the constellations in the sky. They will have covered almost 40 miles (64 km) by the end of the day.

At last they stop to camp for the night. They unload the camels, tie their legs so they won't wander off, and feed them their daily meal of hay. Then they gather around a campfire and roast one of the goats they

have brought along for food. A mixture of goat cheese and ground millet rounds out the meal.

In the flickering firelight, they joke and tell stories as they savor rich Tuareg tea. They speak of the old days and of the hardships and poverty of modern life. And they ponder the future of the Tuareg in these harsh, uncertain times.

Traditionally, the Tuareg are seminomadic camel herders who live at the desert's edge. Their homes are open structures with hides across the top. A group moves to another site when their camels need fresh grazing ground. Although Agadez is the Tuareg capital, most of the wealthy merchants there are Hausa or Fulani.

The *azalai*, or salt trade, is still the realm of the Tuareg, as it has been for hundreds of years. About 1,000 camels make the trip every year, compared to many thousands per year in the past. Some men bring their young sons along on the trek to teach them the routine.

Wodaabe Ways

The lives of the nomadic Wodaabe revolve around their herds of long-horned Zebu cattle. A herder is deeply attached to his animals and knows each one by name. When a new calf is born, it's given two names—one name after its mother, and a second name for some physical trait.

Men are responsible for cattle herding, political affairs, and planning their group's migrations. Boys begin tending cattle at an early age. Girls help their mothers milk the cows, gather firewood, and make the daily meals.

Young Wodaabe nomads

On this table next to her shelter, a Wodaabe woman displays signs of her wealth.

When the group reaches a new grazing area, the women set up their households. All the wives of one man arrange their separate homes around a central space. Home is a shelter with a bentwood frame covered with cloth or hides. Inside is a bed of mats supported by four colorfully painted posts. Outside the shelter, each woman sets up a long table to display her prized possessions—dozens of calabashes nested inside one another.

Shame and reserve are central ideas for the Wodaabe. No one should ever gaze directly, or gaze too long, at another person or thing. This shows desire, and desire is embarrassing—a source of shame. It's more dignified to be reserved. That same reserve forbids open displays of affection. A mother, out of reserve, does not call her first two children by their names.

Strange as it may seem, this sense of shame is very beneficial for Wodaabe society. If a man has lost cattle and cannot feed his family, other men lend him cattle for a while. This spares him from the shame of living in poverty.

This man's traditional clothing includes a blue boubou and an embroidered hat.

Tuareg girls dressed in their finest clothes for the Cure Salée festival

A man's traditional garb is the *boubou*, a long gown in simple white, gray, or brown—or in spectacular shades of bright green or blue. The blue robes and turbans of the Tuareg are dyed with indigo. A well-dressed Tuareg man also wears a finely crafted sword. In their dances, young Wodaabe men wear leather wraps around their hips and black tunics embroidered in rows of colored patterns.

Headgear varies, from small skullcaps to cylindrical white or multi-colored hats. Fulani men wear wide-brimmed hats that slope up to a point or a dome on top. Tuareg men wear a *tagelmoust*—a long swatch of cloth wrapped around the head. Because it keeps the head cool under the hot sun, others besides the Tuareg wear this style. Tuareg men also cover their nose and mouth, considering it improper to expose this part of the face in public.

Women's clothing, too, varies from one ethnic group to another. Many wear dresses or wrapped skirts in solid colors or bright prints. Older Tuareg women may wear dark clothing, while younger women wear wide-sleeved white blouses decorated with bright fabric strips. Wodaabe women

Making Fura

It can take about three hours to make fura. First the woman pounds the grain in a mortar to remove the husks (photo). She rinses the grain, soaks it, and pounds it again to make flour. Then she forms the flour into balls (*dawo*) and boils them for about an hour. The balls go back into the mortar, where she pounds them once again to crush them, adding water to make a mush. With the mush, she forms one or more big balls. One big ball goes into a calabash, where she mixes it with sour milk, more water, and spices.

may wear a striped head wrap and a black skirt with horizontal stripes. They are experts at needlework and embroider their black clothing with rows of colorful patterns.

Food

If Niger had a national dish, it would be *fura*. Fura is a porridge made of millet or sorghum mixed with milk and spices. In rural areas, fura is the main dish—or the only dish—in most meals. Wealthier people add sugar to their fura. Side dishes may include pancakes, salad, fruit, or—in some areas—grasshoppers.

In the south, another common dish is paste and sauce (*tuwo* and *miya*). The paste is thick like mashed potatoes. It's often made of millet, but it could also be made from rice, sorghum, maize, or peas. Sauces might include onions, okra, cassava, or baobab leaves, all bound together with oil or fat.

Taking Tea

Among Niger's nomads, the men often serve tea when entertaining visitors or relaxing after the evening meal. They prepare the rich brew in a pot over an open fire. It's the custom for everyone to get three cups of tea, so more water is added as needed. The first and strongest cup, they say, is "hard like life." The second cup is "sweet like love," and the third cup—the least bitter—is "for pleasure."

Meat is often mixed in. A bowl of paste and sauce makes a cheap and nutritious meal.

Dambou is a traditional village dish that's also sold from the market stalls of Niamey. It's made of rice or millet mixed with the boiled leaves of the drumstick tree (*Moringa oleifera*) and some peanut paste.

Sagai is a steamed dish consisting mostly of leaves. Favorites are pea and sorrel leaves. Many other dishes are made with peas, squash, peanuts, and onions. Flour ground from various grains is also made into pancakes and deep-fried fritters.

Women cook on outdoor fires or in indoor clay ovens. They serve food in calabashes. These gourd bowls, often decorated with beautiful designs, are prized possessions. The lids are round mats of woven fibers.

The Feast of the Mutton

Tabaski, the feast of the mutton, is a great celebration throughout West Africa, and Niger is no exception. Tabaski is the West African name for *Id al-Adha* or *Id al-Kebir*, the

Muslim feast commemorating Abraham's sacrifice of a ram in place of his son Isaac.

As with all Islamic feast days, the date of Tabaski is set by the lunar calendar. That is, it depends on the cycles of the moon. Each year, Tabaski comes several days earlier on the Gregorian calendar—the calendar used in most Western countries—than it did the year before.

Getting ready for Tabaski is an exiting whirlwind of activity, just as Christmas is in Western countries. Markets are crowded as people shop for new clothes to wear, sheep to sacrifice, and food for the festive meal. Even in poor families, fathers splurge to buy new outfits for their wives and children.

Each family sacrifices a sheep for Tabaski. At dawn they wash the sheep, and then the men and boys go to prayer dressed in their finest boubous. Afterward, everyone wishes one another a year of peace and good fortune. Then it's time for the sacrifice. The men kill and skin the sheep while the women prepare for the barbecue.

National Holidays in Niger

New Year's Day	January 1
Tabaski (*Id al-Adha*)	Date varies
Islamic New Year	Date varies
Easter Monday	March or April (day after Easter)
Anniversary of 1974 coup	April 15
National Concord Day	April 24
Labor Day	May 1
Id al-Moulid (Muhammad's birth)	Date varies
Independence Day	August 3
Republic Day	December 18
Christmas	December 25
Id al-Fitr (end of Ramadan)	Date varies

Hausa women dressed up to celebrate Tabaski

The feasting goes on all day. Meanwhile, small children go from one home to another asking for little gifts of money or sweets. In the evening, families go visiting, young people go dancing, and religious leaders offer blessings and prayers.

The Cure Salée

The *Cure Salée* is a ten-day gathering of nomadic clans. It takes place each year in September, at the end of the rainy season. Tuareg and Wodaabe nomads gather around Ingal, west of Agadez, and at other points across the Sahel where the land is especially salty.

Cure Salée means the "salt cure." The rains have brought salts up to the surface of the soil, where grasses soak it up. By drinking the water and eating the grass, the nomads' cattle and camels take in the salt that's vital to their diet.

The Cure Salée is a long-awaited chance for people to get reacquainted and catch up on news of births, deaths, marriages, and changes of fortune. With exuberant music and dancing, they celebrate their culture and renew their sense of kinship and tribal identity.

For the Tuareg, it's a time for parading and racing their camels. Men dress in their finest formal clothes and wear their swords. This is also the time for the *tinde*. While the women sit in a circle singing and beating the tinde drum, the men ride round and round them on camels. One man snatches the head shawl of a woman he admires and rides off with it. The other men chase him down to get it back, and whoever returns with the shawl is the winner.

"We Do It for the Women"

For a young Wodaabe man, the *gerewol* is his chance to win a beautiful girl as his wife. It takes hours to prepare. First, he braids his hair in long plaits, weaving in beads, cowrie shells, and metal ornaments. He dons his embroidered tunic and his finest beaded necklaces and silver pendants.

Then, using a small hand mirror, he applies makeup to accent the facial features that are most beautiful to the Wodaabe. He paints a yellow streak down his nose to accentuate its long, straight form. He uses black kohl as an eyeliner to bring out the whites of his eyes. Kohl lipstick shows off his white teeth. Once his makeup is done, he wraps a long strip of cloth around his head and fastens it with a headband. From the band, he hangs two long strips of beads, shells, and charms. Then he puts on an elaborate pointed hat or glorious ostrich plumes. All this is only preparation for the exhausting ordeal yet to come. But the men are quiet,

serious, and single-minded as they prepare. As one remarked, "We do it for the women."

The men line up in a long row before the women, and the dance begins (photo). Chanting in a hypnotic rhythm, they sway, swing their arms, and dance forward and back, rising up on their toes as they step forward. They roll their eyes, flash their white teeth, and smile as broadly as they can.

The dance goes on for hours, lasting far into the night. When a woman makes her choice, she lets the man know with subtle gestures and glances. When she wanders from the group, the man quietly slips away from the dance and follows her into the bush for a secret meeting.

As soon as they get a chance, the two sneak off to the man's encampment. His family slaughters a ram and eats it to celebrate the union, and then the marriage is official.

For the Wodaabe, the Cure Salée is the time of the *worso*. This is an annual gathering of clans, when hundreds of people make camp together. They perform ceremonies to honor births and seal marriage contracts, and they hold their spectacular *gerewol* dances.

After the festival, each clan goes its separate way. Many matches have been made, though many young men have failed. But they can try again when they all meet the next year.

Different Ways of Learning

Children in rural Niger tend the herds, sell goods in the markets, and take care of younger children. If it's planting time, they plant. If they are nomads, they move when their families move. Some may live 100 miles (161 km) or more from the nearest school. These are just a few of the reasons why school attendance in Niger is among the lowest in the world.

Many children help their families by working and caring for younger children.

A classroom in the city of Zinder

Children who live in cities and towns are the most likely to attend school. Public school is free, and the law requires children to attend from age seven through fifteen. But only about 25 percent of Niger's primary-school-age children actually go to school. Attendance is even lower in secondary schools, at about 6 percent.

Nigerien schools follow the French education system. Primary school lasts six years, from age seven through age thirteen. Children who pass are awarded a certificate. To enter secondary school, students must first pass an entrance exam.

Secondary school lasts much longer than it does in the United States. First comes CEG (*College d'Enseignement Général*), a sort of junior high that lasts four years. After that, students who pass a national exam can go on to *lycée*, a three-year senior high school.

In many villages and towns, devout parents are proud to send their boys to the *medersa*. This is an Islamic school where a religious leader instructs boys in the Koran. They memorize the verses, learn what they mean, and write them out in Arabic script. Thus, they learn reading and writing as they learn about their religion. Many parents send their girls to Koranic schools, too. But as a rule, girl students rarely advance as far as the boys.

It seems almost a miracle that students would ever reach college level. But thousands actually do attend Niger's universities. Abdou Moumouni Diop University in Niamey was opened in 1973. The Islamic University of West Africa—in Say, just south of Niamey—opened in 1987. Unfortunately, the University of Niamey closed when it went bankrupt in 1993, after twenty years of operation.

New Efforts, New Hope

Education levels are lowest among women and girls. Only about 14 percent of Nigeriens can read and write. Among people who are literate, only about one-third are female. Women educators are trying to raise girls' scores on national exams, and their work is paying off. In experimental village schools, record numbers of girls passed their secondary-school entrance exams after these programs began.

Cultural pride is another pathway to literacy. The government has already opened village libraries with books in some of Niger's native languages. Nigerien educators are also hoping to introduce native-language books into the primary schools. For example, Tillabéri would use Djerma-language texts, and Maradi would use Hausa texts.

Folktales and legends, poetry, fiction stories, and humor would be the most likely choices for native texts. The point is to raise interest in native literature, improve literacy in local languages, and encourage reading in general. So richly grounded in their own culture, this new generation of Nigeriens will grow up strong, proud, and free.

Studying the Koran

At a *medersa*, the marabout trains boys in the teachings of the Koran and in Arabic writing. His students gather around him in his house or courtyard for their afternoon class (photo). The marabout picks a passage from one of the Koran's 114 chapters and lectures on what it means. Then the students, sitting cross-legged, copy the verses onto wooden tablets in Arabic script. This helps them learn the verses. They struggle to recite to the marabout what they have memorized before class is over.

When they are teenagers, the boys recite lengthy passages of the Koran before a gathering of men. For Muslim boys, it's a rite of passage. After this ritual, they are considered to be men.

Timeline

	Niger History	

Niger History

A.D.	
Kanem kingdom thrives near Lake Chad.	800s–1300s
Islamic religion gains followers among the Kanem-Bornu and Tuareg.	1000s
Tuareg people move south from Algeria into Aïr Mountains.	1100s
Bornu kingdom replaces Kanem kingdom.	1300s–1600s
Mansa Musa rules Mali Empire, including what is now southern Niger.	1312–1332
Agadez and Zinder are established; Agadez becomes center of Tuareg trade.	1400s
Sonni Ali establishes the Songhai Empire.	1468
Songhai Empire expands.	1500s–1600s
Moroccans conquer the Songhai Empire.	1591
Usman dan Fodio establishes Sokoto Caliphate in Hausaland.	1804
Scottish explorer Mungo Park passes through Niger on the Niger River.	1805–1806
German explorer Heinrich Barth travels through what is now Niger.	1850–1851
French move into what is now Niger.	1880s

World History

2500 B.C.	Egyptians build the Pyramids and Sphinx in Giza.
563 B.C.	Buddha is born in India.
A.D. 313	The Roman emperor Constantine recognizes Christianity.
610	The prophet Muhammad begins preaching a new religion called Islam.
1054	The Eastern (Orthodox) and Western (Roman) Churches break apart.
1066	William the Conqueror defeats the English in the Battle of Hastings.
1095	Pope Urban II proclaims the First Crusade.
1215	King John seals the Magna Carta.
1300s	The Renaissance begins in Italy.
1347	The Black Death sweeps through Europe.
1453	Ottoman Turks capture Constantinople, conquering the Byzantine Empire.
1492	Columbus arrives in North America.
1500s	The Reformation leads to the birth of Protestantism.
1776	The Declaration of Independence is signed.
1789	The French Revolution begins.
1865	The American Civil War ends.

Niger History

Tuaregs rebel against the French.	**1906**
Niger becomes a colony in French West Africa.	**1922**
France allows Niger representation in the French Parliament.	**1946**
Niger's economy booms from good peanut crops.	**1950s**
Niger becomes an autonomous republic within French West Africa.	**1958**
Niger gains independence from France; Hamani Diori becomes president.	**1960**
Niger experiences severe droughts.	**1968–1974**
Uranium is discovered in northeastern Niger.	**1968**
Niger's economy booms because of uranium exports.	**1970s**
Niger's first university opens.	**1971**
Army officers overthrow the government and set up a military dictatorship under Seyni Kountché.	**1974**
Niger's economy suffers because the world price of uranium goes down.	**1980s**
A severe drought causes the Niger River to stop flowing.	**1984**
Tuareg begin a rebellion against the government.	**1990**
Niger adopts a new constitution that allows a multiparty political system.	**1992**
Mahamane Ousmane is elected president in Niger's first free and open elections.	**1993**
Colonel Ibrahim Baré Maïnassara overthrows the government and becomes head of state; Nigeriens approve a new Constitution; Maïnassara is elected president.	**1996**
Maïnassara is assassinated; a new Constitution is written; Tandja Mamadou is elected president.	**1999**

World History

1914	World War I breaks out.
1917	The Bolshevik Revolution brings Communism to Russia.
1929	Worldwide economic depression begins.
1939	World War II begins, following the German invasion of Poland.
1957	The Vietnam War starts.
1989	The Berlin Wall is torn down, as Communism crumbles in Eastern Europe.
1996	Bill Clinton is reelected U.S. president.

Fast Facts

Official name: Republic of Niger

Capital: Niamey

Official language: French

A Tuareg settlement

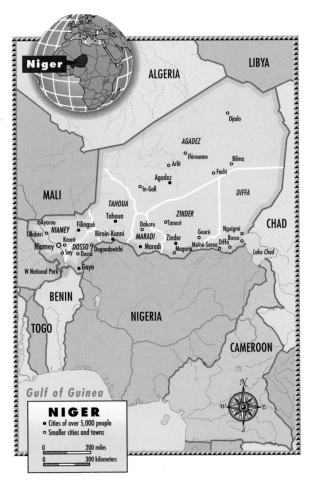

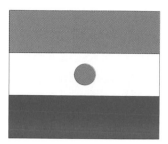

Niger's flag

A mosque in Niamey

Official religion:	None
Year of founding:	As an autonomous republic, 1958; complete independence, 1960
National anthem:	*"La Nigérienne"*
Government:	Republic
Chief of state:	President
Head of government:	Prime minister
Area:	489,191 square miles (1,267,000 sq km)
Dimensions:	Distance east to west: 1,100 miles (1,770 km); distance north to south: 825 miles (1,328 km)
Latitude and longitude of geographic center:	16° North, 8° East
Borders:	Libya to the northeast; Algeria to the northwest; Mali and Burkina Faso to the west; Benin and Nigeria to the south; Chad to the east
Highest elevation:	Mont Gréboun, at 6,378 feet (1,944 m) above sea level
Lowest elevation:	Along the Niger River, at 656 feet (200 m) above sea level
Average temperature extremes:	122°F (50°C) in the daytime in the desert; 32°F (0°C) or lower at night in the desert
Average precipitation extremes:	22 inches (56 cm) in the southern savanna; less than 7 inches (18 cm) in the desert near the Aïr Mountains
National population (2000 est.):	10,800,000

Clay pots in a market

Currency

Population of largest cities:

Niamey	420,000	(1994 est.)
Zinder	119,827	(1988 census)
Maradi	110,005	(1988 census)
Tahoua	49,948	(1988 census)
Agadez	32,272	(1988 census)

Famous landmarks:
- ▶ *Aïr and Ténéré Natural Reserves*
- ▶ *Birnin Quartier* (Zinder)
- ▶ *Grand Marché, Grand Mosque, and National Museum and Zoo* (Niamey)
- ▶ *Grand Mosque, Sultan's Palace, and Vieux Quartier* (Agadez)
- ▶ *W National Park*

Industry: Industry makes up a small percentage of income and of workers in Niger. The main industries are mining and manufacturing. Uranium ore is Niger's most valuable mining product. It makes up 50 percent of the country's exports. Other mining products include salt, coal, iron ore, and tin. Most of Niger's manufacturing takes place in Niamey, Maradi, and Zinder. Important manufactured goods include traditional handicrafts, processed peanuts, millet, and cotton.

Currency: Niger is one of seven West African countries using the CFA franc (*Communauté Financière Africaine franc*). In 2000, U.S.$1=730 CFA francs.

System of weights and measures: Metric system

Literacy: 13.6% (1995)

Djerma schoolgirls

Common French words and phrases:

aujourd'hui (oh-zhoor-DWEE)	today
Au revoir. (o ruh-VWAHR)	Goodbye.
Bien, merci. (bee-EHN mair-SEE)	Fine, thanks.
Bonjour. (bohn-ZHOOR)	Good morning./Hello.
Ça va? (sa-VAH)	How's it going?/ How are you?
Ç'est combien? (say comb-bee-EHN)	How much is it?
demain (duh-MAHN)	tomorrow
hier (yair)	yesterday
J'ai faim/soif. (zhay fahm/swahf)	I'm hungry/thirsty.
l'eau (loh)	water
le pain (luh pahn)	bread
Non. (nohn)	No.
Où est . . . ? (oo eh)	Where is . . . ?
Quelle heure est-il? (kel uhr eh-TEEL)	What time is it?
Oui. (wee)	Yes.
S'il vous plait. (seel voo PLAY)	Please.

Famous people:

Sonni Ali Ber *Songhai king*	(? –1492)
Mano Dayak *Tuareg leader*	(1949–1995)
Hamani Diori *First President*	(1916–1989)
Usman dan Fodio *Fulani religious and political leader*	(1754–1817)
Tandja Mamadou *President (elected 1999)*	(c. 1938–)
Askia Muhammad *Songhai king*	(? –1538)
Mahamane Ousmane *First elected president*	(c. 1950–)

Mahamane Ousmane

To Find Out More

Nonfiction

► Beckwith, Carol, and Marion van Offelen. *Nomads of Niger*. New York: Harry N. Abrams, 1993.

► Englebert, Victor. *The Goats of Agadez*. New York: Harcourt Brace Jovanovich, 1973.

► Hill, Kathleen. *Still Waters in Niger*. Evanston, Ill.: TriQuarterly Books, 1999.

► Koslow, Philip, and Darlene Clark Hine. *Centuries of Greatness: The West African Kingdoms: 750-1900*. Milestones in Black American History. New York: Chelsea House, 1994.

► Ojaide, Tanure. *Great Boys: An African Childhood*. Trenton, N.J.: Africa World Press, 1998.

► Rain, David. *Eaters of the Dry Season*. Boulder, Colo.: Westview Press, 1999.

► Seffal, Rabah. *Niger*. Cultures of the World. Tarrytown, N.Y.: Benchmark Books, 2000.

Folktales

► Addo, Peter Eric Adotey. *How the Spider Became Bald: Folktales and Legends from West Africa*. Greensboro, N.C.: Morgan Reynolds, 1993.

► Arkhurst, Joyce Cooper. *The Adventures of Spider: West African Folktales*. New York: Little Brown, 1992.

► Courlander, Harold. *Cow-Tail Switch and Other West African Stories*. New York: Henry Holt, 1987.

► Ugorji, Okechukwu K. *The Adventures of Torti: Tales from West Africa*. Trenton, N.J.: Africa World Press, 1991.

Internet Sites

▶ **Africa Speaks**
http://www.uic.edu/classes/engl/
engl161-patstoll/afspeaks.htm
*A collection of stories by Nigerien
students about growing up in Niger.
Includes topics such as customs,
rituals, family life, rural life, and school.*

▶ **Focus on Niger**
http://www.txdirect.net/~jmayer/
fon.html
*Links to a wide range of information
on Niger, including current events,
ethnic groups, and human rights issues.*

▶ **Kids' Almanac: Niger**
http://kids.infoplease.com
*Choose "countries," then enter
"Niger" in the search window for
Information Please Almanac's
children's page on Niger.*

Embassy

▶ **Embassy of Niger**
2204 R Street N.W.
Washington, DC 20008
(202) 483-4224

Index

Page numbers in *italics* indicate illustrations.

Meet the Author

ANN HEINRICHS fell in love with faraway places while reading Doctor Dolittle books as a child. Now she tries to cover as much of the earth as possible. She has traveled through most of the United States and several countries in Europe, as well as the Middle East, East Asia, and Africa—including Niger.

"Deserts are my favorite terrain," she says, "especially empty ones. They're so clean and mystical. In the Sahara I felt refreshingly small and insignificant." What were the highlights of her stay in Niger? Sleeping on the desert floor, gazing up at the starry sky, listening to folktales by the flickering firelight, sipping Tuareg tea, cradling a newborn baby goat in her arms, and camping and dancing with the Wodaabe.

Ann grew up in Arkansas and lives in Chicago. She is the author of more than thirty books for children and young adults on American, Asian, and African history and culture.

"To me, writing nonfiction is a bigger challenge than writing fiction. With nonfiction, you can't just dream something up—everything has to be true. When I uncover the facts, they turn out to be more spectacular than fiction could ever be.

And I'm always on the lookout for what kids in another country are up to, so I can report back to kids here."

Two of Ann's Children's Press books—*Australia*, in the Enchantment of the World series, and *Louisa Catherine Johnson Adams*, in the Encyclopedia of First Ladies series—were first-place award winners in the National Federation of Press Women's communications competition.

Ann has also written numerous newspaper, magazine, and encyclopedia articles and critical reviews. As an advertising copywriter, she has covered everything from plumbing hardware to Oriental rugs. She holds a bachelor's and a master's degree in piano performance. These days, her performing arts are t'ai chi chuan and kung fu sword.

Photo Credits

DATE DUE

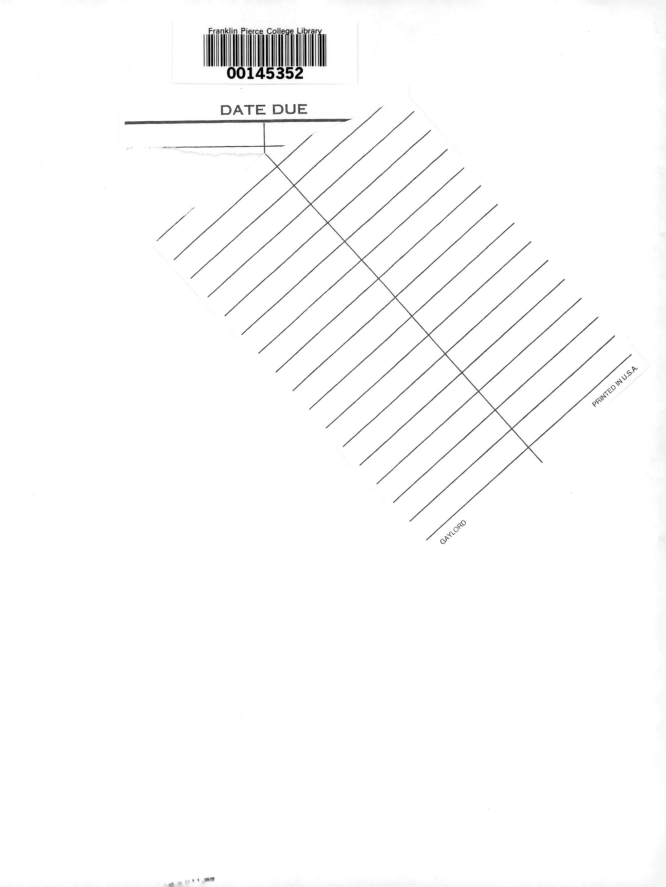

GAYLORD

PRINTED IN U.S.A.